David Sutch, BA (Hons) PGCE, has been an advocate of Magic and associated practices for over 30 years. During that period he has undergone training in Ritual Magic, Druidry and Wicca. He has used that training to practical and personal effect and is now living a simple life aboard his narrowboat, Beith, from where he administers and runs the Anam Cara School of Natural Magic.

About The Anam Cara School of Natural Magic

The Anam Cara School of Natural Magic was established in 2014 by David Sutch to be a centre of training for those drawn to the ideas presented in this book and as a wider community of like-minded individuals.

To Join The Anam Cara School of Natural Magic

First of all read this book and, if you are interested in taking on its practice, book a place on the Foundation Course. This will usually take place at a centre in Nuneaton in Warwickshire. The course takes place over one full day and will add further detail to the ideas presented in this book, as well as giving you an opportunity to meet like-minded people and ask any questions you may have regarding the system. Membership will then depend on mutual agreement. You need to be happy with us and we need to be happy with you.

Membership will allow you access to our Facebook community and access to further workshops and events.

All workshops are personally presented by David Sutch as the school does not allow others to present its ideas in any form. Any workshops not taught by David will be in contravention of copyright and therefore illegal.

To book onto our Foundation Course please find details on our website at

www.anamcaraschool.co.uk

Natural

Magic

A Guide for the 21st Century Practitioner

David Sutch

Published by Rosestrum Publishing

This book is dedicated
to the memory of

Tom Sutch

Acknowledgements

To my partner, Louise Ward, for her unerring support in the writing of this book. For the hours of reading and discussion as each part of the text unfolded.

To Leanne Fitzpatrick for creating digital versions of the graphics, the design of the cover, editing and her support in creating the Facebook groups and blog pages for The Anam Cara School of Natural Magic.

To all those who have attended and supported the Anam Cara Workshops. The discussion and feedback from those workshops has proved invaluable in the writing of this book.

The Anam Cara School of Natural Magic

This book has been designed as a manual in support of the work of the Anam Cara School of Natural Magic. It contains a system within itself based on easily understood principles. Beyond the basic practices it has the potential to empower the practitioner towards the development of a personal magical path.

Anam Cara is a Celtic term meaning 'soul-friend'. The philosophy of The Anam Cara School of Natural Magic founds itself in that context. The Anam Cara School is about people and connections with like-minded others and Otherworldly energies. It is a supportive environment, both materially and non-materially, and it offers sanctuary for those seeking alternatives to the mainstream.

The Anam Cara Way is about working towards a magical way of being using the advantages we have in 21st Century culture. Never before have the gates been more open, but we need to re-evaluate our lifestyles and challenge the values of our education. We need also to reconnect with a side of our being which has become neglected.

The Anam Cara Method of Natural Magic is specific to The Anam Cara School. It has been developed by David Sutch as an accessible means towards a magical and productive way of being. The method itself is outlined within these pages and is supported by a full range of talks and workshops.

The Anam Cara School is based around the Midlands and our full range of courses and workshops can be accessed from our internet pages. Should you wish to find out more about our work contact David by connecting to The Anam Cara School of Natural Magic.

www.anamcaraschool.co.uk

Contents

Section Three
The Cauldron and the Wheel

Section Four
The Magic of Beyond

Introduction

This book has been written as a manual for The Anam Cara System of Natural Magic. The system is based on traditional principles, but is a development in that it has been designed to work as a system suited to the 21st Century way of being. We live in an age of information with levels of personal choice beyond the scope of virtually any social group in history. We have a social structure which allows high levels of individuality, and there are various lifestyle choices we can make to enhance the way of being we have the potential to achieve. In other words we can be exactly who we want to be. However, the reality for many is a high level of social control. We are constrained into a world of stressful work patterns to afford high housing costs, debt and a cycle of "want" based on the constant lure of consumer products which are pushed upon us by TV, advertising and internet search engines. This book has been written to support those free spirits who seek something beyond.

We live in an age of unlimited information, where individuals can be as they want to be rather than constrained by traditional community expectations. We can be as geographically mobile as we desire and create ourselves in any image which pleases us. We are wealthy; whether you agree with that statement or not, simply by the fact that we live in a major Western capitalist economy, which means we have more wealth than any social group hitherto existing on the face of the earth. We only 'feel' poor because we choose to pay out so much in order to support what can justly be described as 'excessive' lifestyles.

The word 'choose' in this context may cause a few frowns, so let us think about it a little: We choose where we want to live, we choose a lifestyle to suit our expectations, we choose the car we want to drive, we choose the supermarket we shop at, we choose a career, we choose how much TV we watch and we choose how to spend our money. It can be argued however, that the choice is probably influenced by expectations placed upon us. We have grown up in a capitalist society with capitalist values, whether we are aware of them or not. We are educated to believe in the value of hard work and the rewards it can bring. We value the materialistic side of life and we seek to secure as much as we desire in the form of consumer services and products. We are rich by any standard. The nobles of the past may have had huge hoards of money, but unlike us, they did not have a vast array of products to spend it on. Until Medieval times no one even had glass windows!

If you are looking for a magical guide to becoming wealthy in material terms, this is not the book for you, but if you desire a greater variety of choice in your life and a means to discover a lifestyle that works for you, then please read on. The Anam Cara System is about bringing Magic into your life, it is about re-evaluating your place in the world and the expectations placed upon you by the society in which you live.

The Anam Cara System is about Magic. Not romance or illusion, but real Magic. But what is Magic? To our ancestors, magic was matter of fact, very much an aspect of daily life, a superstitious belief system for some, and a way of being for others. It was something many, such as the Medieval Church, felt the need to protect against. For others it was a fascinating world of enchantment to aspire to. Witches and Cunning Men were often seen as those with innate abilities, special people, gifted with second sight, otherworldly people or maybe those who were just a little bit different. However, this world view changed during the period of 'enlightenment', when science became the dominant driving force in its quest to understand and control the natural world. Magic ultimately became discredited as superstition. That said, even though magic has lost its credibility in the wider belief system of mainstream culture, it has always remained as a real potential within the minds of the few. It is for those few this book has been written.

Over the Aeons a huge amount has been written about magic and magical systems are present, in some form, in virtually all societies. There is probably nothing new that can be written about magic. Regardless, magic remains elusive, ethereal and transcendent. In the study of magic today we have access to a huge body of literature and records of practice from cultures of all descriptions. Never before has such a wide diversity of source material been so freely available. It could be argued that we now have the opportunity to work out what it actually is in order to be able to work with magic effectively.

On the other side of the coin, it could be argued there is too much source material. There is a confusion of systems and we are actually spoiled for choice. We can be purists and opt for one or another, or take the postmodern road and pick the bits we like from each. Either way it will take a great deal of time and dedication though it will be later rather than sooner when we will have enough experience to evaluate our chosen route. In my own experience many systems were tried, but never yielded the results I sought. In fact it would be more accurate to say I never really knew what results I was actually seeking. However, the journey was interesting and I learned a good deal on the way. With hindsight I am now able to consider how I would like to have learned with the experience I developed in my studies. I would have benefited from:

- A cohesive system based on traditional, well-tested techniques.
- The potential of support from others working within the same system.
- A system based on clear, easy-to-understand principles
- A non-dogmatic practice in which to develop personal preference.
- An experiential path which would work in accordance with modern standards of life.

In this book I have attempted to produce a system based on the above considerations. It needs to be worked as a system within itself in the early stages, moving towards the goal of achieving an energy flow within the Whole Self. Once this has been achieved you will **know** something inside you has shifted. This is a natural form of initiation. Initiation here is not conferred as recognition of following a prescriptive programme of study, but as a Self realisation that will occur naturally. It is rather like learning to play a musical instrument; there comes a point when it moves beyond a learning curve and becomes a natural practice. Beyond that initiation, it is important to develop and follow your own chosen path, which will be an organic and natural progression. The energy flow within the Self will create its own momentum.

In a meditation some years ago I made a connection with the Celtic God, Cernunnos, and I was given the challenge to find, *'the fixed point of stillness'*. I have found it in many places to my comfort, but none more so than in this theory as it is from a fixed point that the Anam Cara System builds into a cohesive, integrated Magical construct to build a flow of natural energy within the Self. I realise through working on this book that *the fixed point of stillness* is a beginning and not an end. I mention it here by way of introduction; however I would point out that you may not really understand what I am saying until the end, such is the conundrum! Please just bear with me.

A fixed point has no value within itself as it is only a point, but build around it an equilateral triangle with the fixed point at the centre and we have a beginning; we have a centre around which the three angles can revolve. We can then enclose the triangle in a circle to demonstrate the potential of flow. Take it one stage further and draw a square to enclose the circle, and beyond that create two more circles. The Whole is pictured on the front cover of this book and is called the **Rosestrum**. It forms a visual image of the theory through which the Anam Cara System works. The story of it will unfold as the book progresses, but hold it in your mind as a focus. Everything about the Anam Cara method is contained within its structure.

It should also be noted here that this is an experiential path, hence it has been important to include examples of my own experiences and realisations, as it is around these happenings that my own understanding is based - *these sections are included in italics.* I hope you enjoy and benefit from the practices suggested in this book and that you also connect with the practice, as without experience there can be no Magic.

The Rosestrum.

The image of the Rosestrum is central to the understanding of this book. It is original and exclusive to the teaching of the Anam Cara School and has been designed by the author to enable clear understanding of the text. Within these pages you will find a coloured postcard of the image for use as a visual aid as you progress with the system.

15

Foundation

*Magic is subtle and elusive. It can be near, but always just out
of reach. It is as alluring as a beautiful fragrance whose scent
we catch momentarily. It is a twilight world, where fleeting
shadows catch the corners of the eyes. We know it is there, but
we can never quite grasp it. It is enchantment itself, but once
we have tasted it, it calls to our souls.*

Magic **is** real. It is matter of fact and attainable. It is attainable
only to few, not by the need for any special qualities or
inherited birthright, but by the time and effort it takes for an
individual to make it work. The people drawn to it **know** it is
there and seek to find it. Of those who seek it only a few will
find it in its pure form. There is no elitism about this as Magic
is fleeting and exists beyond grasp. Even when it is found it
comes and it goes depending on our needs. It is enough,
however, to bring it into our awareness and to bring it into our
lives as the foundation of a way of being. It is enriching,
enticing and enchanting. It is Magic.

The following story relates to a Magical experience of
my own. It will also give you a little background as to where it
is I am coming from.

I experienced Magic in its pure form on a narrowboat during the period between Beltane and Yule in 2010. It was a very lonely period in my life.

I had retired from work and been through a transformation in my lifestyle culminating in the move from a house to a boat. I had also lost my youngest son to suicide. It was a devastating time. After many years of searching for magic through comparative religion, philosophy, esoteric societies, Rosicrucianism, Hermeticism, Ritual Magic, Wicca, Druidry and a whole range of alternative literature, I was at a point where I had a good understanding of what I needed and how to attain it. Though, I have to say, even after all of those years of study, I never truly experienced Magic I was seeking. It was a very important part of my lifestyle, I could use magical means to make things happen. My world was open and I was filled with expectation, but it was all about effort, it was my Intention that made things happen and I had largely mastered my fears, but I hadn't let go, I hadn't allowed Magic to really take hold, I was in control of my life and I was not letting go. Real Magic, I was to learn later is about connection and flow. It is experiential and it happens in its own way. It cannot be forced and it cannot be mastered.

My journey on the boat began in the summer. I was alone with my thoughts and my thoughts were dominated, absolutely, by the death of my son. I was out in nature twenty four hours a day, walking miles to keep my serotonin levels up in order to be as hormonally happy as I could possibly be. I was out each night watching the sky through the side hatch of my boat taking joy in the beauty of the stars.

17

*I was meditating every day for hours at a time. I was taking myself into different worlds which were becoming more real to me than the one I was in. I was encountering things I had never encountered before and I developed a very strong feeling that I was being looked after. By whom or what I do not know, but I **know** I was being looked after, I could not doubt it.*

Winter came early that year and while I was moored near Napton locks in Warwickshire, the ice came and froze me in for six and a half weeks. I couldn't walk much at that time as the ice made it difficult and it was so cold I took to my bed, buried in quilts and blankets, where I carried on with my meditations and connected with things that profoundly influenced me. The experiences I had through those months were so clear they cannot be put down to coincidence, but I came out of it and moved back into the visible world before I became lost in an alternative world of inner vision. This shift was also a part of my sense of being looked after. I feel now that I had been nurtured, but it was time to bring me back to reality for my own sake. The powers that were brought me a chance meeting to bring me out of it.

I am still processing it now as it was so intense. I came out of the experience with a sense of wellbeing and a very different understanding of life and death. I connected with things that remain with me, but the intensity of the Magic has passed for now. Magic is much more a part of my lifestyle than before, but the power of my need for it has reduced.

*I still feel the magic, but I don't need it in the way I did. I **know,** however it will be there when I need it again. Because of my experiences I am back in control of my life and now I feel led to teach and to pass on the understanding of Magic I* *achieved from the many years of study and my depth of experience during those months in my cocoon.*

    This book has grown out of those experiences and is an attempt to understand the mechanisms by which Magic works. However, we need a beginning. Look at the Rosestrum again and you will see a triangle. Triangles have three corners and to each corner we need to apply an idea leading us to the next section: This will be our starting point.

Three Principles of Natural Magic

The three principles of this section relate to the triangle at the centre of the Rosestrum. On the left is the symbol of the Sun, on the right is the symbol of the Moon and at the top is the symbol of a spiral of Energy. These three symbols form the beginning of the Anam Cara System of Natural Magic building out from the *fixed point of stillness* at the centre of the triangle itself. In the first instance each concept needs to be understood as a thing within itself, but the goal is to integrate the three concepts into one and to create a flow of energy around that immutable point.

The three principles are as follows:

1. **The Sun** - There is a material self; (Masculine, the Visible World).

2. **The Moon -** There is a non-material self; (Feminine, the Unseen World).

3. **The Energy Spiral** - There is an Energy that connects everything in the Universe.

   There is nothing complicated about this, but knowledge of each of the concepts requires its own understanding. The idea is to examine each one in detail and to work practically towards giving each its own reality **within yourself.** It is an exercise in the development of consciousness.

The Sun

The World of the Material Self

The material world is a masculine place. It is our visible reality, a logical construct governed by the laws of nature. It follows clear, universal principles and is a matter-of-fact place to be. It is seemingly undeniable, but this undeniability needs to be challenged. The Visible World may not be the place we may think.

We all know the world of the Sun much better than we understand the other two worlds of Moon and Energy because we are always aware of it. We have a body, and that body dominates our consciousness and way of being. It is the vehicle by which we function in life. Many of us see this world as all there is. Our belief systems, however, have been cultivated in that way by the society in which we live.

We live in a materialistic world dominated by the ideology of science and have done, as a society, for the last four centuries. Science, as a belief system, is deterministic in that it determines the way the majority of us think by virtue of the fact that we have been educated within a scientific

22

paradigm. It describes the world as a place where all can be explained and ultimately controlled.

The world of our ancestors was more a place of wonder, where supernatural explanations were a means for human life. It was also a place with an unseen world where fantastic things had the potential to happen. Science has overridden the enchanted world of our ancestors by disputing ideas that cannot be 'proved' and in doing so has effectively closed the supernatural aspects of ourselves which do not fit within this structure. It has made us into what can be described as one dimensional beings; that is, beings with the capacity to function in the material world, but rarely beyond. Science has created a material path and as the Piper, it expects us all to follow its tune.

Human culture has developed over thousands of years and we have a rich history of ideas and cultural models, but the track we have taken in the Western world is towards increasing materialism. It is a road without turnings, taking us all in a single direction whether we want to go there or not. Science has linked itself inextricably with economics and the two have created a world of technology linked with finance. It is a world of material possession with the soul of a microchip and the promise of nothing but more of the same.

Economic considerations control our lives, and it is through science that technologies have developed to provide an endless stream of new products to feed the ever hungry economic system. It controls both us and our thinking and ultimately makes us into passive consumers rather than the architects of our own existence.

We have little control over the lives we live as we are constrained by mortgages or high rents and expectations which are far beyond any other cultural group in history. In other words, our lives are planned for us and we have precious little by way of alternatives. We need somewhere to live, we need water, electricity, gas, food, clothes, entertainment, transport, and all of the other trappings of material life, and it has to be paid for. The vast majority of people struggle to meet those expectations and our lives are dominated by stress, debt, addictions, depression and the modern diseases that follow from the effects of those conditions. This has been summed up in the concept of 'Affluenza', a book by Oliver James. If you earn good wages you can be 'happy', but if, like the majority, you don't, what has materialism to offer you? It is a single track way of being with little space for personal choice.

Whilst this book offers no solution to the problem of these constraints, it does offer a potential to develop a lifestyle within the dominant culture. This can help to minimise the effects of materialism on the self and provide the basis of a holistic way of being which ultimately leads to a greater degree of personal satisfaction.

The Moon
The World of the Non-Material Self

The non-material world is a feminine place. It is our invisible side, a non-logical construct, not governed by any laws of nature. It has its own principles and is nurtured within its own unlimited nature. It has none of the limitations of the material world, but is a world of magic and deep potential. The Moon represents the side of ourselves we need to cultivate.

The non-material self is less easy to know than its material counterpart. It is not manipulated by social forces in the way of the material self, it is usually just ignored and undervalued. It has fallen away from us over the centuries and it needs to be revived. There are many words that can be used to describe the non-material self; perhaps it is the spirit, the soul, the subconscious or unconscious mind, or maybe it is the human essence or ego. It doesn't matter. There is no need to examine or theorise about what it is, the point is to **experience** it, whatever it is, and allow it to return to life.

The words 'non-material self' are used here because of their neutrality, as preconceived ideas can often lead to misunderstandings. We are talking here of the inner world most commonly accessed in the form of dreams and less commonly in the practice of meditation. It is a fragmented world, difficult to understand and even more difficult to interact with. It is possible, however, to provide the non-material self with a 'structure' by which it can communicate on deeper levels with the conscious self. It can be understood as the mediator between universal energy (the top point of the triangle) and the material self. This connective, when employed effectively is a real means by which the Self can be experienced as a whole being.

Connecting with the non-material self is not an overnight task, it requires time and dedication, but time is not easy to find when we spend so much of our conscious energy on the demands of material life. Therefore we need to work effectively to limit the power of the material self in order to create the space we need to explore our non-material side. The egg, in this case, needs to come before the chicken.

Beyond that it becomes possible to create a structure within the non-material self through meditation. This is not the meditation of clearing the mind of thought as practiced in Eastern methods, The mind does however need to be cleared of superfluous thought in order to create a free flow of energy within the images conjured by inner journeying. Most of the intrusive thoughts affecting meditation will be to do with the concerns of material life, so the methods outlined in the work of the Cauldron (later in this book) will be essential to the success of this practice.

Look again at the illustration of the Rosestrum; if we were to drill a small hole in the top of our triangle and pass a loop of thread through this hole, it would hold itself in balance if held by that thread. This is the goal we need to set for ourselves, as these two aspects, the Sun and the Moon, the Masculine and the Feminine, need to be held in balance if we are to experience the Self as a unified whole. Too much on one side or the other will create an imbalance within the Self.

There is an Energy Connecting Everything in the Universe

This is the topmost point of our triangle. It is the third principle. There are perceivable energies in nature. Trees have energies, as do animals, birds and plants. There is also energy of place; different places 'feel' differently, as do people; some we are drawn to and some we prefer to distance ourselves from. The Anam Cara System treats all of those energies as one unified whole. The aim is to animate the Self (the triangle) by infusing it with the energy of nature.

This is the most abstract of the three principles, but also the most powerful. This is an energy which has become neglected in Western thought, but it exists. It can be perceived and it can be worked with on the journey towards a sense of completeness within the whole self. It cannot be quantified in an empirical way, so is of no value to the materialistic philosophy of science. It is however central to the theories of quantum physics, which are now becoming popularised in both literature and film.

Imagine the natural world and everything in it as a web of energy in which everything is connected. Imagine it as a huge spider's web and if one strand is plucked the vibrations reverberate around the web just like the ripples from a stone thrown into a pool. It cannot be seen, but it can be perceived by the non-material self. It is a feeling rather than an actuality. That is the heart of the theory on which this book is based.

By working, using visualisation and inner connection, this energy can vitalise the non-material self. In turn, the realisations achieved will influence the physical self. But, it does not end there. Energy, in the form of the natural world, will make itself known in the physical realm to the material self, taking the form of coincidence or synchronicity. These realisations then feed back to the non-material self to reinforce the experiences and to validate the effectiveness of the flow. This has to be experienced to be believed, but it will happen if the exercises in this book are practiced successfully.

Achieve this and you will be at the beginning of Magic, but only the beginning. There is much more, but this is an initiation, a deeply personal initiation, meaning that your life will never be the same again. Once this is experienced the world will be a different place.

This energy has the potential to flow through the non-material self and be realised in the material world. This, in turn, will feed back into the flow of energy itself. **It is essential to understand the significance of this triangle before moving on** as it is absolutely central to The Anam Cara System.

The aim is to achieve an energy flow as an actuality feeding from energy itself into the non-material side which will then manifest within material life and accordingly feed back into the primary energy field, thereby influencing its patterns. The following chapters will concentrate on the practicalities of creating that energy flow.

To summarise: the goal is to create a balance between the material and the non-material self, which correspond with the energies of male and female respectively. Once that balance has been achieved it is possible to connect with the non-material side with the energy that flows within nature. From here you can create individual patterns within the energy flow towards manifestation within the material self.

Section One

On the Art of Creativity

*The Magic
of the
Material Self*

Earth in a Barrow

The silence of the soul of the past
Locked away in weathered stone
Chambers of solitude
Fading in darkness
Tempting with secrets
Depth of earth, solid and stable
Knowing but silent.
Loosen the chains, leave them to rust
Deep in the Barrow

Reflections in Earth from West Kennet Long Barrow
the day after leaving work.

David Sutch July 2008

The Sun and the Magic of the Material Self

Magic is a potential on the material level within itself and this is the Magic of Creativity. Human beings are born to create just as birds are born to fly. Creativity exists on various levels in terms of thought, action, emotion and manifestation.

The material self has a Magic of its own, which is not dependent on anything other than itself. This is the Magic of Creativity and it works by making the material side of the self as creative as possible. This is about making things happen, but it is also about creating ideas, lifestyles and potentials. One of the best examples of this is the creativity stimulated by the shortages of World War Two when need created responses in people towards making their lives as good as they could possibly be, by making the best of what they had. The imagination of it all was incredible and those who lived through it have fond memories of this time. This is because they were alive with ideas and creative responses during a time of terrible adversity. They really did learn the potential of what it is to be human.

The Anam Cara Way is the way of experience. Everyone is different and we all have our own paths to follow, so there is no one single mode of practice. We all have values and expectations and very often they are tied into social expectations. On the other side of the coin, we may dream about ways of life which offer alternatives, but are unable to connect them with them due to the practicalities of the lives we have. It is good to be aware that alternatives are attainable and creative lifestyles are possible. Social constraints can be overcome and the support of like-minded people can really help. Our lifestyle choices can only be our own however, so no prescription is possible. Below is a description of my own lifestyle choice and my reasons for making it.

Personally, I feel the need to live on the fringes of mainstream culture, because if I get too much involved in it I become drawn away from the magical life I have developed. It is about choice. For me, living on a narrowboat is perfect. I am out in nature virtually all of the time. I have no TV, but I do choose to take in the odd film and I do tune into the radio, so I have some awareness of what is going on around me, but not too much. I keep myself busy, enjoy good friendships and ultimately I just go along with what I feel like doing at any particular point in time.

Simplicity is important to me, as the concept encapsulates my value system as a whole, and this is just as well as life on a narrowboat is very basic. Water comes from stand-pipes, toilets need to be emptied and heavy bags of coal need to be carried, sometimes for long distances. If my life was more materialistic and complex I would need to work to earn the money to pay for it. As it is I don't spend much, so I don't need to work too hard. This means I have time, though not much money. I find this preferable to having money and no time, which is what I would have if I had to work long hours.

Because I have time, I can create for my needs, which means I don't need to spend much on purchased goods. Being on a boat in a small space means I cannot just accumulate stuff, so recreational shopping is off the list as meaningless practice. I do however enjoy elegance and a pleasant living environment and I love good food, so life is not without its luxuries by any means. The idea of 'simple pleasures' is central to me as that is what life is all about and to me this is a Magic within itself.

Here the work is about challenging the materialistic emphasis of the consumer lifestyle. Whether you take it on is up to you, but it is a sound basis from which the value of this system can evolve. In order to develop the connection between material self, non-material self and energy, as outlined earlier, it is important to simplify. This does **not** mean going without, quite the contrary, but it does mean adjusting your relationship with consumer ideology. Buy less and make more is the general principle here. It is about creativity and its relationship to self awareness.

Creativity is empowering. It is hugely satisfying to create for your needs rather than to rely on passive consumerism. It is also an important part of the human essence or what it actually is to be human. Creativity becomes an aspect of your identity and relates to self esteem. The act of creating builds on itself and quickly becomes a way of life. To be around the things you have made is a constant reminder of how talented you can be. It is addictive, but in a good way.

The act of creating is Magical. It begins with an idea and that idea may then become manifest through the process of creating or the making process. To make something requires time, and the time you use is a part of your life; therefore a part of your life goes into the thing you are making. The finished artefact actually becomes a part of you, a part of your being. It will become a thing that is and will necessarily contain a part of your energy or life force. The more you put into creativity the more you will realise your own potential as skills develop over time and the creative process becomes a natural extension of Self. This is true Magic as the art of Self realisation.

Consumer consciousness denies us this satisfaction and it is also very expensive, both in terms of time and money. By following the ideas in this section you can shift your awareness. How far you take it is up to you, there is no formula but the ultimate aim is to play down your material self and increase your basic sense of worth. Work at it and it will also cost you significantly less to live, thus giving you greater choice over how much of your labour you need to sell.

If you can cut down on working hours you will have more time to concentrate on your creativity and your non-material self. It is possible to live an empowered life even within the confines of consumer society. Creativity is not just about making things it is also about lifestyle. Creative lifestyles mean alternatives and a sustainable way of life is a significant step towards the development of a Magical way of being.

The Art of Frugality
Creating a Magical Lifestyle

Recently there has been a great deal of interest in simplicity as a lifestyle choice. People are increasingly concerned about overconsumption, environmental issues and economic uncertainty. It can be argued that the society we live in is unsustainable as it is based on the overconsumption of natural resources and there seems to be a resistance to the development of sustainable alternatives. We are not in control of our economic circumstances as a nation. It is governments and multinational companies that dictate the direction of technology and they are locked into oil, only paying lip service to the development of alternatives.

If the peak oil thesis is correct, we are now at the peak of oil consumption meaning that supplies will dwindle in the none too distant future, challenging the fundamental basis of the world economy. The recent banking crisis is testament to the fragility of the financial world and the lack of responsibility in which it operates. Apathy on the part of banking executives was clearly the cause. Think about it, if the banks had gone down how would our lives have been affected? If oil supplies decline, how will we adapt to a life we are unprepared for?

The culture we live in has made us dependant rather than productive. The wages we earn are probably higher than at any time in our history, so we can buy pretty much what we want and if we cannot afford it, we can have credit. There is no reason for us to cater for our own needs because it is quicker and easier to use retail. There is no material need that cannot be bought, there is always a plentiful supply to keep us wanting more, and new products are constantly being generated. It can even be said that we are trained to want from a very early age by relentless advertising and social expectation, but what is the alternative?

Society is structured in such a way as to make it difficult to live outside this accepted norm. The bottom line is that we need to meet the bills and there are always plenty of them to pay, so simplicity is not simple to achieve. The more we earn as a nation, the higher housing costs rise, add to this the expense of council tax, rising energy prices, TV license fees, telephone and broadband, insurance, transport costs and the wealth of other expenses that eat away our earnings. How is it possible to live simply in a culture like ours?

Simplicity can mean living with greater awareness, looking for cheaper or less packaged alternatives and engaging in practices such as recycling. It can mean going one stage further by taking greater responsibility for creating our own lifestyles. I stumbled on this, through need, back in the 1970's and it has had a profound effect on my life ever since. It is a very difficult idea to explain as really it needs to be experienced. To me it was like an enlightenment, which had an effect on every aspect of my life, both then and now.

My introduction to what I call the 'Art of Frugality' grew, out of necessity in my twenties when I found myself alone with a baby to bring up. Sole responsibility for a baby without any family support was a daunting prospect leaving plenty of room for creative thinking. I had very little and could not work, so our only income was from social security, just enough to cover the basics. We moved into a flat which was cold, with minimal furniture and few home comforts. There was a cooker in the kitchen, but nothing else, not even running water; that had to be carried up from the ground floor. We lived on the third. This situation, however, brought out the best in me and it was quickly transformed into a happy and comfortable lifestyle.

The first task was to provide heating. There was a boarded up chimney, but no fireplace, so I lifted some large quarry tiles from the back yard and set them in cement to form a hearth. The chimney was opened up, but there was no fireback. Fortunately the area I lived in was being improved, so many of the houses were being renovated. Talking to builders got me a free, used fireback, a grate and a damper which I fitted easily, on their advice and without prior experience. To finish it, I needed two lengths of angle iron to provide a trim between the fireback and the wall and I got this from an old bedstead found in a skip. I bought some pine boards to make a surround, which was simply made and cost me just six pounds (1970's prices). The fuel we used was wood and there was plenty of it in skips for free. We were warm and the whole process took little more than two days.

The flat was carpeted, but it was badly worn. I cut out the best bits and made a patchwork with some carpet samples I had bought for not very much and it looked quite funky. The floorboards around the edge were left exposed and painted with some leftover paint I was given. There was a worn out three piece suite, unpleasant to sit on because it was so old, so I bought a quantity of denim jeans at a jumble sale for a few pence each and I unpicked them and sewed them onto the suite. All was hand sewn with a needle and thread, so it took quite a long time, but it was worth it; it looked really good when I had finished and there were pockets everywhere for keeping bits and bobs.

Shelves were put in the alcoves using the best of the firewood I found and the room was painted with a large tin of budget priced white paint. The cost of the whole process came to less than £20. The rest was made up from bits of furniture I had found in skips or bought from second hand shops. All was restored into my own style with basic repairs and paint. The flat was transformed into a comfortable and stylish place to be. Nowadays this is called 'shabby chic', but back then it was borne out of necessity and just plain common sense. More important was the effect it had on me. In the most adverse of circumstances I was positive. Because I was positive, I was empowered and because I was empowered I was in control of my life and that control made me happy.

I had a bicycle with a seat on the back for my son so we could travel freely. We ate simply but well. All of our food was fresh and cooked from scratch (because we had no fridge). I got the bug for this and went on to do everything for myself, making bread, making wine from things I could pick and saving every possible penny I could. At the end of each week there was money left over and each week I would measure my success by trying to increase the amount I could save. We always had all we needed and there was money available to give a sense of security. We had a lifestyle that was not really *any different from anyone else in that we ate well, had a comfortable place to live, transport and places to go, but above all, we had quality time together and no stress.*

I learned many new skills and felt happy and successful, so much so that I had the confidence to go back into education after leaving school with no qualifications. Over two years I gained 6 'O', and 3 'A', levels and a place at Warwick University to study Philosophy and Sociology. We moved to Coventry and rented a house, which I furnished on the same principles. However this was the 1980's and my frugality went against the norm of the time; which was all about making money. The Eighties prompted a major shift in consumer ideology with privatisation, home ownership, yuppie lifestyles and the massive expansion of the retail sector. I responded by being myself and becoming a toymaker, specialising in Victorian type, kinetic wooden toys, but making a business of it didn't really suit me so I had to sell out for a while and join in, albeit reluctantly, with mainstream culture.

I ended up in teaching, where I stayed for 20 years, but I could never leave my frugality behind, so my lifestyle always remained relatively simple. Consequently I ended up with a modest house with no mortgage and enough savings and pension to allow me to live comfortably for the rest of my life and I was able to retire at 53. Now I have choice and I have returned to my frugality, which again empowers and inspires me. Since then I have downsized to a narrowboat where I now live, what I consider to be, the ultimate life of freedom.

In talks I have given about simplicity the questions are always about how to make it possible. Of course it is possible, it can be done but it does require real dedication. It is about awareness and a totally different approach to life. It is about creativity and positive thinking. It is also about overcoming the mindset of want and creating new attitudes towards what it means to be alive. My frugality now is different to the frugality I had, but I still see it as an art. Once that art has been mastered it becomes a lifestyle of immense satisfaction and self sufficiency. My own baptism was through adversity so I learned it the hard way, once I achieved realisation of how empowering it really is, I could never leave it behind. Because of my experiences I am now a free spirit with, hopefully, a great deal of stress-free life still to look forward to.

If you can identify with this experience you may be interested enough to develop a simplistic lifestyle. The following ideas might be useful to you:

- Make an honest list of all of your outgoings on an annual basis then divide it into monthly and weekly amounts. Then work to reduce them by finding the best deals and switching providers. After that, rewrite your list and see how much you have saved, it will probably be a considerable amount. Working on annual figures, £5 per week becomes £60 per year making a worthwhile saving so always round it up to annual totals.

- Treat utilities as the precious items they are and reduce your consumption to the absolute minimum. I halved my water bill by having a meter fitted because I am consistently frugal with water. Heating is the biggest expense so wear warmer clothes rather than turning up the thermostat.

- Don't buy new. Get over the idea that second hand is second best and seek out your needs at car boot sales, charity shops and eBay or better still, create for your own needs.

- Look after what you have. Things such as household items can always be improved with few materials and a little imagination. The wartime idea of 'make do and mend' really applies here.

- Evaluate your food consumption. This can be a major saving by avoiding processed foods and cooking fresh ingredients from scratch. It is also possible to simplify what you eat avoiding the cost of expensive ingredients.

- Don't buy anything you don't need. We all fritter away money on a daily basis, newspapers, bars of chocolate, lunches at work and the like. Getting into the habit of making sandwiches each day saves a considerable amount in itself.

- Evaluate your social life. A good social life need not cost much and there are cheaper alternatives. Instead of an expensive night out, what about a good night in with friends?

- Make for your needs rather than buying; it is far more satisfying once you get into the routine.

- Work out how much your hobbies and interests cost. To the true adherent of simplicity, hobbies should be craft based and productive either for need, to sell or to give as gifts.

There is nothing new here and the list is by no means complete, but it is all common sense. If taken on as a package you will be amazed at how much you can save and you will find that your values and expectations will also change. Instead of taking pleasure from buying things, take pleasure from providing for yourself by your own ingenuity or by tracking down the things you need as used items and buying them cheaply. In time the level of satisfaction increases and simplicity as a lifestyle becomes self perpetuating and, correspondingly, your bank statement becomes less difficult to open.

Considerations for the Affluent

If you can afford to support your lifestyle then why bother to be frugal? In my experience frugality gives you control over your circumstances and increases your personal choice, particularly in the long term. Significant improvements can be made in quality of life for yourself and your family as a whole. Consider the points below as examples of what you may be able to achieve:

- Use your savings to pay off your mortgage early giving you the prospect of freedom later in life.
- Living simply may mean that you can work part time as you will need less, or in the case of two parents working, one could stay at home and use the time productively. This will lead to a less stressful lifestyle and improve quality time with children.
- Develop your skills and creativity.
- Lead an environmentally friendly lifestyle as a natural consequence.
- Use the time you create for yourself for personal or spiritual development.

- Retire early while you still have the energy to develop new potentials.
- Use your savings to cover a career break or retrain to escape a job you find stressful.
- Take on a lesser paid job that you will enjoy rather than staying in a job that may be meaningless for you just because you need the money.

Again, the list is not complete, but you will see that frugality is not just a thing in itself; it may also have significant impact on potential lifestyle choices. It can be life changing. All of this is difficult to take on alone as you will be going against the norm. Unless you are particularly strong with a great many abilities you will need the support of others around you, so developing group or community support is important to success. This is a central philosophy of the Anam Cara School and there are people out there who seek to simplify and who are willing to offer guidance and support to you as you start out.

To practice the Art of Frugality successfully it is important to develop effective support networks, because no one person can have all of the necessary skills required. It is important also to find like-minded people to work with and support you because this lifestyle goes against the norm. Encouragement, new ideas and moral support are all essential to success. For this purpose the Anam Cara School Facebook site has been established. Use it to contact like-minded individuals and take on the practice of skill sharing. Like for like reduces the need for money in exchange and you have the satisfaction of shared energy.

Elegant Simplicity

A way of life without illusion,
Beyond the mainstream, a way of its own.
Based on a fusion of honest simplicity,
Practical elegance, colour and tone.

Toxic Western culture likes control.
Culture with no heart and with no soul.
Advertising makes you want to own.
Everything you are is what you're sold.

Break away now by refusing to pay
The dues required for subscription to Mammon.
Break the addiction, the inbuilt infliction,
Of culture intent on enslaving its own.

Moving forward around the Wheel
Learn what is good and learn what is real
Break with the past to embrace what is new
A path that is open, but only to few

Create the solutions to all of your needs
Build on your talents and work as you please
Take on the challenge to create your being
You now have the choice, so do it with feeling

Nature is a storehouse of interest and need
Free to all participants and generous indeed
All of the beauty you'll ever require
There for the taking, don't pass it by

Innovate and speculate, don't set any limits
This is a life that's dignified and sanctified with spirit
Take away the limitations, take away the strife
Elegant simplicity means quality of life.

David Sutch 2009

47

In a Nutshell

The Art of Frugality is not about going without, but an alternative to conventional consumer lifestyles. It is perfectly possible to live a life of greater quality on considerably less. You can have all of the benefits, but less of the cost by using your imagination and abilities rather than your wallet. Ultimately it may free up more of your time by allowing you to work fewer hours. It benefits individuals, family life and communities. Most importantly, it develops creativity and positive thinking towards a low impact and stress reduced life

Simplicity and Reconnection

If you choose the path of simplicity and work with it, it can be taken further and deeper into the Old Ways and the realms of enchantment. The following essay sets the context for a 21st Century understanding of Natural Magic and the practice of the exercises that follow will begin the experiential nature of the work.

After twenty years spent teaching Philosophy and Sociology I find it hard to leave it behind, so a little theory needs to creep in at this point. I was inspired here by John Michael Greer in his book 'The Druid Magic Handbook'; the argument is about disenchantment and the fact that the world we now inhabit is a very different place from that of our ancestors.

Max Weber, a German social theorist, postulated theories about social structures in the light of improvements in the lives of the masses beyond the Industrial Revolution. He argued that Western society would develop into a rational structure based on bureaucratic principles. He also recognised that society would necessarily become disenchanted and that religion would fall into decline.

Before scientific materialism seized the imagination of Western culture, people saw the world around them as a place of Magic, where trees and stones could speak, birds traced out the future in their flight and those who knew the secret could sense and shape the flow of enchantment in the world around them. He had no belief in magic itself but used the metaphor to express the extent of the differences between the two worlds.

Whilst Weber did not lament the loss, there were others who did. William Blake for example described the new industries as 'Dark Satanic Mills', and expressed his own dissatisfaction through the medium of art and poetry. John Ruskin and the Arts and Crafts Movement recognised the consequences of mass production on individuality and promoted the virtues of traditional skills and handmade production. A wealth of artists and visionaries adhered to these principles and began a backlash. Though influential, could not prevent the development of the factory system. This was also the time of the revival of Druidry due to its real connection with nature and the energies of the Earth.

Weber, however, stood the test of time. The backlash was of the period, and Druidry from its promising roots, became synonymous with Freemasonry, where it remained until the latter half of the Twentieth Century. Magic itself remained and developed in the late Victorian era with the Theosophical Society and the Hermetic Order of the Golden Dawn at the forefront of the revival. The history and practice of Western magic was synthesised into cohesive systems particularly by the Golden Dawn, and eventually fed through into the public domain when previously secret doctrines were published. This opened the gates to those who would otherwise have had little access and, in part, gave birth to early forms of modern Wicca and similar practices. This however is High Magic, the initiated traditions open only to the few, but what of traditional practices? Folk magic had been practiced for many centuries by simple folk, witches and cunning men; what of this?

It can be seen here there are two major magical traditions, the initiated magical elite and the simple folk practitioners. Folk practitioners were seen as those with second sight, herbalists and healers, those who could curse and lift curses, witches who could affect weather; go to sea in eggshells; shape-shift into crows, hares and cats; fly on broomsticks; commune with the fey and enchant the wary and unwary alike. They were feared as their powers were universally accepted to be real in a culture where magical belief was as real as out of town shopping centres are to us. However, the power grew from universal belief in the reality of magic and the mystery of the practitioners themselves.

To find out about these practices we have a wealth of information in the form of folklore, herb lore, recipes for flying ointments, an understanding of the psychology of curses and the like, and it is not actually difficult to reproduce the practices. What we cannot reproduce is the belief system that went along with it and it was the belief system which truly enabled the power. In our modern, rational society much of the power of folk belief has dissipated.

Natural Magic is about Enchantment in a dis-Enchanted world. It falls more naturally on the side of folk tradition due to its simplicity, and may incorporate aspects of the initiated tradition, but it has to be a magic for the 21st Century rather than a relic from the past. It gains its power from its relationship to the culture of which it is a part. In this case, it is the power it has on the individual rather than the collective, but it does gain from collective practice.

In the past it was witches who were marginalised. The traditional place of the witch was the last house in the village, indicating a physical separation between the witch and the community. In the present it is those with odd ideas that go against the mainstream that arouse suspicion. Living a life that is different is not easy to do and never really has been. It is possible to work on the self and create positive lifestyle choices, but it is always good to meet with like-minded people to gain approval and support, hence the power of the collective.

Researching the practices of the past is easy to do; we have search engines. It is not purity of knowledge we need to seek as much of what you find may be questionable. However, we do have the ability to cross reference and to read between the lines. The belief system before industrialisation was supernatural in nature and not necessarily acceptable to the modern mind, so again, it will need to be interpreted. If you have ever tried flying on a broomstick or changing yourself physically into a hare, you will quickly realise it is not possible in the scientific context. Nature is ordered and works by its own principles; so we, in the modern world, will need to find Natural Magic rather than working in the realm of superstition and, if we take the trouble to look for it, we will find that it is still there. We have the power of imagination, so if we develop this faculty within ourselves we may discover an Otherworld where anything is possible. The superstitions of the past may be the keys to magical realisations in the present.

A good example of this is the world of the Fae. Read into folklore and you will find that the rural areas of the past had a sophisticated understanding of 'Themselves'. Folklore is abundant about the ways and means of living alongside the Realm of the Fae - how to protect yourself; the ethics of interaction; ways to please; things that must never be done and a wealth of tales about people who have fallen foul or have been helped by the Sidhe (pronounced 'shee', meaning the faerie realm). We can find details of whole hierarchies, places where They dwell and details of individual characters such as Jenny Greenteeth, Peg Powler and Redcap.

But where are They now? We have Them in children's stories and films, but we don't take precautions around Them any more, as we don't tend to accept Their reality. However, this is what Natural Magic is all about, reconnecting with Enchantment. Read about Them and allow Them to enter into your consciousness, find wild places and sit with the intention of seeking Them. Wait until twilight and look for Them in the shadows. You will not find Them in your living room, so go out and seek Them. Hawthorn trees in full blossom seem to invoke Them as does the Rowan. They are there in bluebell woods, which are full of enchantment, if you **allow** yourself to feel it. But take mind to cut two Rowan twigs and bind them into a cross to hang over your threshold as once you know They are still there, They will know that you know!

The past is gone, but the enchantment is still there and there is a wealth of tradition waiting to be tapped into. The reality is in the imagination and it is through imagination we can experience the wonder of it all.

Practical Exercises

Towards reconnection with Enchantment

1.   Read folklore and traditional fairy tales, but don't just read them, imagine them. The development of imagination is central to the ways of Natural Magic. Having read the tales a few times try to recall them in a meditative state and live through them. Be a part of the tales in your inner vision. If you tell anyone what you are doing they will think you are "away with the faeries" - and you will be!

2.   Research into the traditional meanings attached to animals, birds, trees, stones, herbs and flowers. There is a vast body of folklore attached to the natural world. In traditional societies they had storytellers, but we have search engines! A bit of technology does not go amiss.

3.   Go out and visit special places; woodlands, sacred sites and country places. Take a picnic and stay out late, but go alone or with people who seek the same as you. Try and tune into the energies of these places, it is not difficult, but it will be

if you spend your time chattering! Try the Rollright Stones on the night of a full moon, it is pretty well impossible not to feel enchanted there.

4.   Try to tune into the energies of different tree species. Find ones that naturally attract you and sit with them. What kinds of feelings do they invoke in you? Keep notes about this exercise and visit the same trees at different times of the year. You might notice subtle changes in their energies

5.   Be aware of energies that are around you in your everyday life. Enchantment is in everything, if you seek it.

6.   If these practices are taken on you will begin to notice changes in your consciousness. Your inner world will begin to become Enchanted.

The Magic of the Material Self

Magic is multi facetted. In this book four types of magic are considered; the Magic of the Material; the Magic of the Non-Material; Natural Magic in the form of the Cauldron and the Wheel and, finally, the Magic of Beyond. Each of the four will be discussed in their own sections, but here is the place to discuss the potential of the Material Self as a single entity. Magic exists on various levels and is enhanced as it develops, but it can be understood as the Magic of a material process within itself.

We have discussed the idea of simplicity and the concept of reconnection with Enchantment. Now we need to put them both together. By evaluating your own material life and making conscious changes, the relationship you have with your physical self can be enhanced in order to develop feelings of deeper satisfaction and positive self esteem. This is a Magical process in itself as it involves transformation. It is very easy to get stuck in the physical realm by adhering to old habits and remaining in your comfort zone, but when values are questioned and alternatives considered, physical change can take place and may form the basis of wider self empowerment.

It is important to begin the Magical path by challenging old patterns in order to bring new energies into play. It has been argued here that modern society and its value system creates individuals with materialistic attitudes and expectations and that the deeper aspects of Self, that once were a part of what it is to be human, have been denied to the detriment of the human condition in the 21st Century. It is desirable now for anyone wishing to develop a Magical path to challenge those values in order to set the material foundation for growth.

Your material circumstances are your own, and it is not my place to be prescriptive, however there are various conditions that are more conducive than others to the development of Magical connection. Too much adherence to material values is self denying, in that individual control over personal satisfaction is minimized due to the expectations placed on you in both work and social situations. By living up to expectations you deny the expression of personal qualities that could lead to greater levels of individual satisfaction. By increasing levels of personal satisfaction you will automatically gain greater control over your circumstances, and that is the foundation of the self confidence required to bring about deeper understanding of the needs of the Self.

Erich Fromm, in his book 'The Fear of Freedom', argued that from a psychological point of view, individuals have the potential for freedom but are intrinsically afraid of it. Fromm argues freedom is isolating, and within that isolation, insecurity replaces the sense of belonging. In other words, we simply do not want to be different and we will do exactly what is required to be accepted.

From a sociological standpoint, it can be argued that we are conditioned from an early age to accept the limitations society places on us. We are educated to conform, and the social control mechanisms of law, media, education, work, family expectations, peer group pressure and the needs of the economic system all conspire to keep us in our place as 'functioning' citizens. Magic, however, requires that for individuality to function, it needs differences as it is only by removing the social overlays that we can begin to know ourselves.

When we begin to develop an understanding of ourselves we begin a process of self empowerment, but what is it we **really** want out of life? How many of us can answer that question honestly, outside of the social expectations we are conditioned to respond to? The only means by which to realise this facet of ourselves is to shift beyond those social expectations, but this is not easily achieved. The only suggestion I can offer here is to simplify. It is only through lowering our expectations and weaning ourselves off social conventions and consumer culture that we can experience an alternative and it is only by experience that we can understand and assess where it can take us.

Living on the boat, my partner and I get by with the simple life and are quite happy just to enjoy the peace and quiet. We live out in nature and have the never ending entertainment of the wildlife to keep us occupied; along with the company of good friends. After a while it becomes a way of life and nothing is missed. Time is spent being creative. My partner has taken up crochet and has become really good at it and will sit for hours making all sorts of things. Cooking is usually from scratch and life is simple. A whole range of

58

things go on around the boat. A good friend of ours has made some seriously good cushion covers for the dinette and is just about to embark on new curtains in exchange for my gardening efforts. Another of our close friends is in the process of doing all of the artwork on the outside of the boat to bring it up to its ethereal best. Some media talented friends made a truly brilliant video of a recent trip we all made, this is a must see and can be found on You Tube as, 'A Life Named Beith'. We move about to stay in different places and generally enjoy life. I earn a little from the Tarot and the Natural Magic courses I teach and life is sweet. When I compare my simple life with my previous highly paid teaching job, there is no comparison. We live now on very little, but do not need any more because life is simple and that's the way we like it.

There are so many benefits that grow from the simple life. Stress, for example, was once a standard feature of my daily life as a teacher, but is now almost completely absent. This has really positive long term health benefits, along with significant increases in personal happiness. There is greater understanding of my inner self as there is no longer any pressure on me to do anything I choose not to do. I do exactly as I wish now and I have the freedom of Self determination.

Financial affairs are insignificant in the scheme of things, so there are no money worries to keep me awake at night. There is so much time available to me for creativity and that, in itself, is life enhancing regardless of what it is you choose to create. The knock-on benefits of this are self discipline, increased self confidence and enhancement in personal energy.

There is a real sense of personal empowerment within simplicity. Have you ever noticed when things are not going well that life has a tendency to get more difficult? It becomes an uphill battle; the experience of wading through treacle. When money is needed the bills come rolling in. Nothing works and nothing flows. However, when life is good, everything seems to work together, luck attracts luck, though difficulty attracts difficulty. Some writers call this, 'the law of attraction', and in certain circumstances it does seem to hold. I would not call it a 'law' as that implies universal application, but there is a grain of truth here.

If it is possible to get on top, it is easier, by default, to stay on top simply because more of your life will be sorted, leaving less to go wrong. This is a desirable state to work towards and is achieved more easily by simplicity than it ever could be by conformity to social expectations and consumer culture. Learn to 'ride your own bike', it is much easier to control than the 'speeding juggernaut' that seems to reflect modern society. It might not have the same power, but it has the advantage of being real and attainable.

But where does the Magic come in? All of this is, in essence, Magical as it involves transformation. Transformation of values, transformation of Self and transformation of circumstances. It may take many years to achieve. I began my path in my early twenties and finally achieved independence at fifty three, so it is not an easy solution, but I still have a great deal of stress-free life to look forward to, so I see it as an excellent investment. It was the price of freedom. Maybe you have the creativity of thought to be more efficient than me - everyone's life is different, so no recipes are possible, but one essential ingredient is a good pinch of steely determination.

There is a danger of sounding a little smug here, but that is not my intention. It all works by degrees. Through my working life in teaching I worked hard both in my job and in my magical studies, but I retained my values of simple living in order to keep grounded and to prepare my way for a very different life. This has now been achieved, but not without a great deal of effort. I was far from free in my working life but with diligence and effort the gateways began to open. My story is only here because I want to show that my theory **can** and **has** worked.

Looking back, I could have reached a state of freedom earlier, but I took the option of security as freedom based on security suited me. In a Sinbad film I once watched there was a saying that has stuck with me and it is one which I use to this day, it said,

"trust in Allah, but always tie up your camel."

Good advice that has served me well. I also have the value of comparison which gives me a yardstick by which I can fully measure the advantages of my new state of being. I begin each day by saying "thank you".

This has been about the material Self. It is only one facet of Self, but even to travel this far can be liberating. There is no need for the complete freedom I aimed for, as all it takes is a reassessment of values and attitudes and a shift towards an easier, more controlled life. We can all achieve this to some degree and it can only benefit those who take it on. Try it, there can be no loss.

On the Rosestrum we are now half way along the bottom edge of the central triangle. In the next section we complete that line. This will be centred on an analysis of the non-material Self.

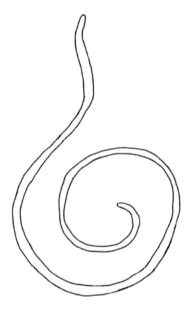

There is an Energy connecting everything in the Universe

Section Two

Of the Art of Enchantment

*The Magic of the
Non-Material Self*

The Non-Material Self

In the 21st Century the average person is significantly better placed to develop a Magical path than at any other point in time. However, we have all but lost this part of our Self, due to the values we live by, which would allow Magic to manifest. To be effective in Magic we need to redress that balance. We need to reconnect with our Non-Material consciousness.

In the first section we looked at the Material Self, its relationship with the society of which it is a part, along with strategies towards developing Magical consciousness within that social setting. The Material Self has become the dominant form of self identity in modern society and necessarily so, given that we live in a 'rational' structure based on the dominance of science and its quest to 'understand' and 'control' nature. As a consequence we have neglected an essential side of ourselves, the Non-Material Self, and have consequently grown out of balance. We have also neglected the Earth and our relationship with nature. It is possible to redress that balance and that is what the Anam Cara System aims to achieve.

To our ancestors, prior to the industrial revolution, there was a natural connection with the Earth; not in the way the more enlightened of us understand it, but a deep connection which was an aspect of everyday life. Before the rise of the towns, the population was largely rural and faced the challenge of living off the land. As such they were subject to the energies of nature in a very real way. They did not have to learn about it in the way we do as it was a natural and practical connection; a part of life and an everyday reality. We are now educated and conditioned towards our own culture, so the experience of being human is actually very different for us than it was for them.

It would be unhelpful at this point to assume a romantic vision of life in the past as a rural idyll, as it was clearly not. Life in the 1600's, according to the philosopher Thomas Hobbes was likely to be, 'nasty, brutish and short', which is probably a pretty fair description. Labour was intensive, incomes low and taxes high and there was a very real danger of starvation. The material side of life, which is so easy for us, was extremely difficult for them. However, theirs was a world within nature, a world of enchantment, which was as normal to them as television is to us. The two sides of life were not separated. The world was enchanted and inhabited by spirits, existing alongside humans. Nature was alive with omens and auguries and people structured their lives around these understandings. Life was not as material as we know it, but it did have meaning and a foundation of tradition as structure.

Would it be desirable to trade our lives for theirs? Probably not, in fact, it would be doubtful if we would last a single winter, we are very soft in comparison to them, so why lament the loss of Enchantment? They may have had their connection to the Non-Material world, but their material lives were difficult. Even the richest of nobles would be poorer in their material circumstances than the majority of us today, given that they did not have the material comforts that even the least wealthy of us enjoy on a daily basis. On the other hand their lives were real and connected more closely to the human in nature than ours. We live in a little window of history, in a life that can be described as artificial and far removed from human experience and its place in nature.

On the positive side we have significant advantages over our ancestors; we have education, sophisticated technology and comfortable material circumstances; but most of all, we have choice. We can choose not to starve to death in the winter and we can choose whether or not we want to reconnect with a side of ourselves that can put us back in touch with the energies of the natural world. We have all of the means we need to make that reconnection, but first we need to overcome our conditioning and realise there is a part of our Self that can be trained to walk again in that World of Enchantment. The downside for many would be the need to move far outside of our comfort zones and to challenge the dominance of our materialistic culture.

The Need to Create Balance Within the Self

The dream was of a passing narrowboat; the top of the boat was grey and the bottom was bright red. On the long foredeck was fastened two large brass searchlights. The name of the boat was Rosestrum.

Imagine the Self as a triangle. At the base there are two angles - on one side is the Material Self and on the other is the Non-Material Self. The two are separate on opposite corners of the bottom line. They are connected by the line, but there is space between the two.

Imagine on the Material side, the symbol of the Sun. The Sun illuminates the Material world. In sunlight we see things clearly; things are as they are. We have the full spectrum of colour and we see things as they are meant to be, and we are unlikely to be mistaken about the things we do see. This is the **real** world.

Now imagine on the Non-Material side, the symbol of the Moon. The Moon illuminates the Non-Material world. However, the level of illumination differs according to the phase of the Moon. The world of Moonlight is very different to the world of the Sun in that it is filled with darkness and shadow. There is no colour and the things we see take on different forms to that of the sunlit world. In quiet places, we feel and fear things we cannot see that hide in the shadows, and we can be mistaken about the things we see as the moonlit world is not clear. This is the **Unseen** world.

Imagine the world of the Sun to be that of the male. It is clear and logical. The rational mind will explain the things it sees as nature can be seen to follow clear patterns. The world of the Moon, on the other hand, is female. It is a world of shadows that stimulate feelings to override logical consciousness. The world of nature may still follow clear patterns, but, in the dark, this is far from obvious. We may know there are no dangers lurking in the shadows, but that will not prevent us feeling them. This is probably why we tend to avoid being in lonely places alone at night!

Whether we are male or female, we will experience both energies even though they are separate. We tend now to live in well lit towns and cities, so the shadow side is limited in our understanding; we have become creatures of the Sun.

Finally, imagine at the top point of the triangle an unseen Energy that connects all things; it illuminates both the world of the Sun and the world of the Moon. It connects everything in both worlds with invisible thread and weaves all aspects of life together into one thing. It is as a spider's web and can be known as the Web of Wyrd. It cannot be seen, heard, touched, tasted or smelled. Science will not accept it as it cannot be empirically proved or bottled. It is of no value, even as a theory, in modern society because it has no cash value. There is no profit to be had from it, so why speculate? So what do we have left of our triangle? We have separate male and female energies and an unseen Energy with no valid proof of existence. The Sun side is powerful, but the rest is pretty useless to our material lifestyles; it will not pay the rent, you cannot eat it and it will not hammer in nails, so why bother to speculate?

Now, look at it in a Magical way. Magic is the antithesis of science. It is the domain of the few free thinkers who can go beyond the norm in order to work effectively within a world view which is opposed to the ideals of dominant cultural confines. It is, and always has been, an individual path, but one which attracts those with the ability to think beyond the visible. It is far more interesting here than it is in the world of the Sun.

Imagine the triangle now as an integrated whole and imagine the whole as the Self. The world of the Moon is as real as the world of the Sun, and there is integration between the energies of male and female. The Energy of the topmost point empowers the Self in all of its aspects and creates a human conduit by which it can express itself in human consciousness. That consciousness, in turn, empowers the individual. This is the essence of Magic.

The Energy is the energy of the natural world. It pervades all things and, whilst it cannot be seen, it can be experienced. The flow is through the Non-Material aspect of Self rather than the Material, hence it is important to moderate that influence and reconnect with our hidden side.

I like to connect with my inner Self early in the mornings. I wake early and find the dreaminess of being just beyond sleep perfect for meditation. I was contemplating the nature of the triangle described above in an attempt to realise its potential. I knew it would need to be enclosed in a circle to symbolise the flow of energy and I also knew that a balance would need to exist beyond, so a square was placed around it to represent the four Elements of earth, water, fire and air. I have long recognised the importance of this balance within the Self and knew it needed to be incorporated. This section of triangle, circle and square represents the Self in its fully functioning and balanced form - the whole Self balanced within the four elements.

However this symbolism is of the inside out, it is of the Self growing into realisation, but there is also an outside in, indicated by the outer rim of the Rosestrum, that is of outside influences on the Self and its place in nature. There are energies influencing who we are and these energies are represented by the heavenly bodies of astrology, the star signs and the planets. This is not all, as the energy of stars and planets, in turn, express themselves in the Language of Nature, the inner language of trees, plants, animals and every other animate or inanimate aspect of nature that may communicate with our inner selves, if we take the trouble to learn that language and listen.

I was excited. At the breakfast table out came my geometry set and my rudimentary knowledge of mathematics, not used since my schooldays, but it came good. Next it was plywood, fretsaw, drill, pots of paint and a big mess (it is not easy crafting projects in the limited space of narrowboats). It quickly came together and I could see it - what was of mind early that morning became matter by the end of the day. My partner was at work whilst I was making it and when she came home, she was impressed. 'What will you call it?' she asked; 'A Rosestrum' said I, triumphantly. I hadn't thought about it at all, but I remembered my dream of the narrowboat from a few days before because I was intrigued by the name. In my dream the top of the narrowboat was grey (passive, feminine, of the Moon), the bottom was red (active, male, of the Sun) and the two brass searchlights to represent Energy - the Energy of nature and the spiral. It was my triangle. I just love synchronicity and to cap it all, the boat of the dream was in full flow!

Grounding in the Elements

The importance of grounding when taking on the practice of Magic cannot be overemphasised. The types of Magic used in this system involve a release of Energy from the Self into the energy field of nature. If the Self is ungrounded the direction of that Energy will be affected. Imagine a hosepipe with a flow of water, under pressure, flowing from it; when it is held it can be directed and the flow will be under control, but let go of it and it will take on a life of its own. In the same way when working Magically, a fixed point from which to work will create a more reliable flow.

But what is grounding? Feet on the ground, practical, not taking off on flights of fancy, earthy, fixed....there are many descriptive words and phrases, but in the Anam Cara System grounding refers specifically to balance within the elements. To the Ancients there were four elements, Earth, Water, Fire and Air. They are not equivalent to what we understand as elements in the form of the periodic table, and they are not a dinosaur consigned to the dustbin of history; what they are is a profound understanding of the nature of human energy.

Look at the image of the Rosestrum and you will see a triangle at the centre, representing the Self, ringed by a circle which, in turn is enclosed by a square. The square is painted four different colours as each colour corresponds with two of the eight festivals. The circle is the Wheel of the Year and is itself rooted in the elements. Samhain and the Winter Solstice correspond with Earth; Imbolc and the Spring Equinox with Air; Beltane and the Summer Solstice with Fire and Lammas with the Autumn Equinox located in Water. These are fixed points that cannot be changed. The Triangle of Self in the centre of the Wheel can move; each point of the triangle can point to any of the festivals and this is as it should be as the human, in its empowered form, has the potential to express any of the energies of the Wheel of the Year within its own sphere of existence.

Let us now concentrate on the square. It is coloured brown for Earth; yellow for Air; red for Fire and blue for Water. It surrounds the triangle of the Self and, due to the balance of the geometry, it holds the centre of the Rosestrum in symmetry. While the triangle can move within that symmetry it is itself held by a fixed point at its absolute centre. This, I refer to as '**the fixed point of stillness**'. It is from this point everything else can revolve as it represents the very centre of being; the grounding point. It is the Self balanced within the elements and working in harmony with the Energy of the Wheel of the Year. It is also the triangle of the empowered Self, balanced between its Material and Non-Material aspects enabling the flow of Natural Energy within itself.

This is exactly what is meant by 'grounding' in the Anam Cara System. The Self needs to connect and hold itself in balance within the energies of the Earth and also to balance itself within the elements. As there are four elements, a good analogy is a four legged table. Imagine a table of solid oak with each leg representing a different element; if the legs are out of balance the table will not stand true, but in balance it will be solid and stable. The same is apparent for the well balanced human, but that balance requires work on the Self in order to achieve and maintain stability.

The Four Elements

The Ancients divided the world into four Elements; Earth, Water, Fire and Air. Everything in both the Material and the Non-Material worlds could be understood using these principles. In Magic these four elements are the composition of Self and the natural world, and just as the old alchemists sought to alter the properties of both the natural world and the inner world, we need to do the same. There is a fifth element of Spirit which will be discussed later, but for now four is enough. The following categorisations are important to understand.

Earth is the grounding factor. It is to do with the Material self, money, work and creativity. Earthy people are often homely, enjoying good food and comfortable material surroundings. These people can be hard to budge due to their need for a sense of security in all things. They fit with the astrological signs of Taurus, Virgo and Capricorn.

Water is about emotion, dreaming, intuition and, in contrast to Earth, it is about inner realisation. Watery people are emotional feeling people who would often be drawn to the caring professions and they are people who usually have a strong sense of family. Astrologically, the water signs are Cancer, Scorpio and Pisces.

Fire is transformative; it is to do with action and making things happen. It also relates to passion. Fiery people are the entrepreneurs, the people who initiate things and create new potentials. Astrologically, the fire signs are Aries, Leo and Sagittarius.

Air relates to thought and communication. It cannot be seen, but is always there. In the form of thought it can be formative, but it needs to be actualised in order to manifest. Airy people can often have their heads in the clouds or they might become great thinkers or public speakers. Astrologically, the air signs are Gemini, Libra and Aquarius.

To test out the effectiveness of these categories try to attribute them to friends, family and acquaintances. Some people are obviously well grounded making them earthy or they may be emotional, watery people. It is usually the case that the most dominant element in a person will manifest in their personalities, some may be on the fence between two or more elements, but this is less common. Then, if you know their Sun sign check it out with the lists above. Think about the element though before the sign, you will be surprised how often they fit.

When you get the feel for the elements try a little self analysis and work out on a scale of 1 – 10, how much of each element is present in your own makeup. I found myself to be very strong in air and weak in fire; I could think for England, but rarely acted on any of my thoughts. This realisation raised my awareness, so now I consciously make things happen to balance the elements within myself. The goal is to work on each of the four to create a true balance, but the reality is that it cannot be consistently achieved as life tends to get in the way. However, the objective is there and the process of being conscious of the need for this balance leads to a significantly more balanced approach to life.

The qualities of the elements are also present in the natural world. Each is a naturally occurring form and nature itself can be divided into the categories of the four to correspond with the elements, but there is a further division that can be applied. Fire and Air are traditionally associated with active male energy, while Earth and Water compose passive female energy. Do not get too tied up with the gender associations as male and female here refer to energetic qualities rather than stereotyped sexual identity. By accepting these descriptions as being of themselves we can apply the qualities to the natural world in order to employ it effectively in our workings.

Hence we arrive at the potential of male Magic and female Magic. If you have made a connection with the Druid Craft Tarot deck by Phillip and Stephanie Carr-Gomm, through our workshops, you will relate to the foundation of male Magic within the understanding of the Magician card while female Magic is encapsulated in the archetype of the High Priestess. This is the basis of the Magical system postulated within these pages in the form of Cauldron work (female) and the work of the Wheel (male).

The triangle of Self set in the Wheel of the Year within the balance of the Elements

The Tools of the Elements

Tools are not essential to the practice of the Anam Cara System, but sometimes things can just be desirable. The tools suggested here cost next to nothing, are fun to make and highly evocative when used. Principally, they are made of wood and slate and they correspond to the four elements.

Earth: this is a circle of slate about nine inches in diameter with a painted pentacle.

Air: is represented by the knife or athame, which has a blade of slate and a piece of tree branch crafted into a handle.

Fire: to represent fire we have the wand or wands. These are just simple lengths of specific woods whittled to form wands. See the section on Ogham for the meanings and uses of different woods for different Magical purposes.

Water: to represent water you will need a chalice. I have always had it in mind to make one and I have tried turning one from wood as well as painting glasses, but I always go back to the first one I purchased, which is a silver plated cup I bought in a charity shop for £2, it is the only money I have spent on my elemental tools.

Slate is easy to find, either in builders skips or reclamation yards. It is soft and it cuts easily with a coping saw. Finish the edges with a rasp or a file or maybe chip a rough edge with a small hammer. Wash well when finished and coat with a little vegetable oil to bring up a bit of a shine.

When engaging with the practice of the Cauldron and the Wheel (later in this book) it is good practice to set up an altar on which to centre your efforts. An altar is an expression of the elemental balance you will be seeking to achieve. Creating your own tools will give you a focus and a structure around which you can work.

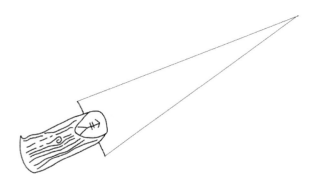

A Slate Athame

Connecting with the Non Material Self

This connection needs to be developed by meditation, visualisation and listening. It is important here to be clear about the type of meditation which is most effective to practice within this system. Eastern systems of meditation are based on the practice of stilling thought, the art of non thinking. With a Western mind, it is very difficult to effectively take on this practice as we do not have the cultural background as a basis for success within this practice.

Consider instead the practice of stilling the mind in terms of the worries, cares and difficult memories that usually occupy our consciousness during times when we are naturally quiet; such as the early hours of the morning when sleep is evasive. How many of us can avoid the worries of the day when we are searching for sleep? If you can concentrate on a particular train of thought at times such as this and allow your mind to focus on a specific theme, you can meditate; but if you cannot, you have work to do.

This work is about changing troublesome thought patterns by physical means. The Cauldron and The Wheel are specific methods associated with The Anam Cara System, but any method to do with positive thinking would be appropriate.

The idea is to clear the mind enough to be able to meditate without intrusive thoughts getting in the way. This will be an ongoing practice as new worries always grow to replace old ones, but with effective methods to deal with them, the process becomes easier and meditation begins to flow. Without the ability to still the mind effective meditation will be all but impossible.

Meditation, in the Anam Cara System, is the practice of liberating the mind enough to allow trains of thought to express themselves clearly without the intrusion of unhelpful thought patterns. This is the most effective way to connect with the non-material self.

Section Three

Natural Magic

The Cauldron and the Wheel

Working with the Cauldron
The Magic of the Moon

Moon Magic is the Magic of the feminine in the Anam Cara System. It is protective and nurturing. It is about reflection and the transformation of Self. Within the Tarot it is represented by the archetype of The High Priestess. This Magic is intuitive and contained within the transformative nature of the Cauldron.

How is it possible to restructure the mind? How can we effectively deal with troublesome thought patterns? There are various ways, usually involving high levels of self discipline, but the one presented here is a little bit different in that it uses the methods of Natural Magic and the Old Ways as a means to alter patterns of thought and replace the negatives with positives. It is about working with the Cauldron as a means of transformation. It is about creating brews on an individual basis to revisit and revise old patterns of thought. The thoughts most invasive are often the negative ones, so what better than to create new relationships with them using the power of Traditional Magical techniques.

This is entirely personal as you will need to create your own brews for yourself, there are no recipes. However, in this section you will find suggestions, examples and guidelines. Here you may want to use herbs, oils, incenses, amulets, talismans, poppets, essences or any other methods that may interest you. You will need a book to write it all into and a good sense of humour as laughter is the best method of all. You will also need to keep it quiet, otherwise you may be replacing difficult thoughts with guilty ones.

This section of the work will allow you the means to train your mind effectively and it will engage you on a deeper level with your Non-Material Self. It will also prepare you for the inner work of meditation and visualization. To give you an idea of the effectiveness of this approach, the example below was carried out when I was attempting to open pathways to my distant past. I had traced my family tree back to the seventeenth century where I discovered the name Zouch was an early spelling of my own name, along with a connection with Ashby de la Zouche. I make no claim to be of the original Zouch family, but the association was enough to inspire me into meditation on that line. This would take me back to Brittany and Celtic roots. The following is an extract from my journal.

I was doing some work around what I remember as a poor relationship with my Grandfather. He died many years ago when I was still a child, but the memories remained and kind of got in my way as I was working on opening a channel of energy from myself, at this moment in time, back through to my ancestors. I had already shifted numerous blockages around my parents and childhood memories, but my Grandfather remained. To work on this I took my cauldron and placed in it little things that were representative of him. One was a few threads of yellow cotton as I remember his hair as being stained yellow with nicotine, but when I got to thinking about it other thoughts came to mind so into the pot went representations of all of the memories I could muster.

This was therapeutic in itself as I had allowed myself to revisit old ground despite the hurt. I knew all would be resolved by the end of the exercise. The more you put in at this stage the more effective the outcome.

I then wrote out a statement he made to me which caused a great deal of hurt and cut it into letters and sought to make a new, more positive phrase, however I could not, at that point, think of anything, so I waited for one to come - in my experience this could take a week, a month or a year. There is no point in rushing as it has to be exactly right for it to work and I know when it is right, because I can **feel** it.

Sometime later I was sitting in the boat with my partner watching videos on YouTube when she said randomly "try and find Stanley Holloway". This shifted a memory for me as I remember my Grandfather had a record of Stanley Holloway monologues that I loved as a child. My partner did not know that, but the sheer randomness of it, coupled with my work around my Grandfather made me think his Energy was working through her to say, "hang on a minute, it wasn't all bad!" We used to recite those monologues and laugh our heads off and it made me happy to remember that. Now I had my phrase and I knew it was right... 'Stanley Holloway'... I needed to add a couple of L's to the original letters, but that was okay because it felt right.

There are a few things to note about this. Stuck memories often cloud the reality of a situation as hurtful things cling harder than everyday thoughts and become the overriding memory. In this case, shifting the memory that stuck released other, more pleasant recollections. Also, the impact of synchronicity added to the experience. Why was Stanley Holloway mentioned when he was? It was no coincidence to me as working in this way I have come to expect it. This is the Magic!

The third point is the fact that Stanley Holloway was mentioned by another person who had no connection with my Grandfather, but it is all a part of one Energy permeating all things. To me that was just an aspect of this Energy. Overall it was a result, another blockage lifted and a better memory for me of my Grandfather.

I know you might be thinking I am making too much of this, but be aware that it fits my overall theory and I was able to achieve what I set out to do. If you are sceptical try something similar for yourself, it works.

The final thing to do was seal it, and it seemed appropriate just to burn some sweet smelling incense in the cauldron to send up thanks to my Grandfather. Nothing else was required. I could then work towards connecting with the flow of Energy back to my distant past more effectively.

Working in this way requires creativity on your part as you need to devise your own methods. You have your thoughts and memories and therefore it is for you to work with them. The objective is to quieten the mind of intrusive thought in order to pave the way for effective meditation.

The Practice of Cauldron Work

The reasons for the practice of Cauldron work may be many, but will always involve pain on one level or another. The word pain is used simply to mean a pain that affects our well being in terms of a barrier that may be in the way of our progress. To simplify we can divide pain into two main types, Material and Non-Material in accordance with the structure of the Rosestrum. On the Material side we can make a further division between practical and physical.

Practical issues are of the material world and may stem from the pain of being in debt or, to a lesser extent, around worry over an unpaid bill. In most cases, the material problem will be of a financial nature. This can be addressed by Cauldron work in the long term when associated with the Material simplicity of the first section of this book, but it has to be said that Magic will not immediately pay the gas bill. Financial problems create worry, and worry will affect meditation and visualization, so it will need to be sorted before effective Magical practice can manifest. This is not to say that anyone with problems, such as these cannot work Magic, it just means the problems need to be minimized in order to make them manageable. There is nothing worse than being afraid of the postman.

To begin, work at sorting the problems on the Material plane by striving to get on top. It will be worth a frugal period or longer hours of work for the peace of mind it brings. If your income is higher than your outgoings, even by a penny, you will be far happier than you would be if your outgoings are higher than your income. When on top, stay on top by cutting out unnecessary expense. You can also make this a part of your long term strategies when we move onto the work of the Wheel later in this section.

The second type of Material pain is associated with physical discomfort. This is a far more complex problem than practical issues. Many people are debilitated by pain of this type which will be either medical in character or in some cases, self inflicted as a non-conscious reaction to adverse circumstances. Illness can be understood in this way as a comfort zone, even though it may not be comfortable. I am not making any value judgments here as Cauldron work is around your own being, so the issues and results are yours to determine. Healing is a highly complex art and increasing awareness of the role of mind, body and spirit in the enjoyment of good health is important to understanding the nature of dis-ease. Doctors are far better than magicians in the healing of broken bones, but the practice of Magic can effectively break down energetic barriers which may be deeply rooted in the psyche. Good health should be a primary aim of any practitioner of Magic. If physical pains are present the belief should be that they can be overcome by the practice of Magic. Cauldron work should be directed to counter these issues; however, this does not mean that you should not consult your doctor whilst you work on yourself using the Cauldron!

Non-Material pains are the main focus of Cauldron work as these are the pains with the capacity to haunt. We all have them to various degrees and often they are things we cannot or will not talk about. It may be problems stemming from childhood, overbearing parenting, issues of confidence, bullying at school and the lack of self worth it engenders. It may be more serious in the many forms abuse may take. It could be difficult teenage years, broken relationships or issues around the death of loved ones. Maybe it could involve the workplace and our place within it, but always the energies around issues such as these will be negative and in virtually all cases will involve at least one person, as it is from people that negative energy manifests within our minds.

People create thoughts within us. Often it is of good things, friendship, generosity, humour, love and support. Most people have good intentions and do not set out to hurt, but relationships can also be toxic as many of us will have experienced to our cost. The essence of Cauldron work is about the negative energies relationships such as these create in our thought processes. They have long lasting effects and create energy patterns inside us that may not be conducive to good health, either physical or non-physical. It is these energy patterns of mind that need to be worked on within the Cauldron as they are disempowering in their negative form. Ultimately they may lead to physical health issues and will need to be dealt with, eventually.

*Work with the Cauldron should **never** be about revenge or an attempt to return negative energies back to their source of origin as these are negatives within themselves.*

Never stick pins in dolls or use any form of retribution regardless of how justified you feel, because that will make you of the same ilk as the person you feel the need to protect yourself from. Work instead with positive energy and that is the energy of intention you are creating for yourself. Hone your energy to create positives within yourself rather than wasting it on people who are probably much better than you at sending out the bad vibes.

I cannot stress this enough, malevolent witchcraft is **not** a part of the Anam Cara System as its whole emphasis is towards cultivating a positive flow of energy. Negative thoughts will disrupt the flow and the system will be unable to work effectively as a whole. By the same token Anam Cara is not, 'fluffy bunny'. Cauldron work can be powerful witchcraft, but the work is about **you alone** and the work is designed to shift **your** energy blocks regardless of who put them there. Work effectively and they will become sidelined and powerless to a point where they will not matter anymore. Work in this way and you will affect others, not by sending them bad feelings, but by cleansing your own energy to a point where people will detect it and respond to you accordingly. People will pick up on energies, whether they are aware of them or not, and bright energies will attract bright people. Dark energies, in the same way, attract dark people. However, it is not for me to tell you how to live your life, you need to make your own choices, but it needs to be said that dark energies are not welcome in The Anam Cara School. That being said, let us now get down to matters of Magic!

A Useful Structure for Cauldron Work

1.   Identify a problem. This will not be difficult as we all know the things which affect us. To begin, work with something fairly minor until you can achieve the results you seek. Beyond that, use your formula to tackle more difficult issues.

2.   Decide upon a physical representation of that problem. This will probably be a person or a situation. Build up a profile of the person or situation in your Cauldron and make it your intention to transform the negative energy in your head. The profile can include any indicators of your choice; these may include items such as photographs, nail clippings, hair, any item belonging to or even one that has been touched by the person. It may be that you will write down things that have been said to you that you cannot forget. Anything that reminds you of the person or situation will do. Leave them in the Cauldron while you prepare your positive elements to counter the negative energy. Take as long as you want over this and do not complete it until you **know** you **feel** right about your recipe.

3.   Transform according to your intention. You need to include good energies into the brew. Good energies can be included in many forms. Carry out the transformation in a positive, ritualistic way. Creating a rhyme to repeat over and over is very effective, or in the case of things that have been said, write them down and cut them into individual letters. Rearrange the letters into a new positive phrase and burn the remainder in your Cauldron. Always carry out this process with good intention for yourself, but, do not intend for others, this work is for you and no one else.

4.   Seal your intention. Write out your workings on good paper, illustrate it and include all of the detail. You know when your workings have been successful as there will usually be a synchronicity to confirm it. Then, and only then, finish by sealing it. For this reason sealing wax and a stamp with your initial is useful. On your written sheet make the seal then either keep it safe or burn it. This marks the end of the matter and opens the way to new beginnings.

The situations you will be drawn to deal with will be entirely individual, making it difficult to write guidelines. Go with your instinct, but use the practices of traditional witchcraft as the Old Ways are tried and tested. Nothing is off limits, but the intention must always be positive. **Never, under any circumstances, let it be known what you have done**. If it gets back to the person you are dealing with you can be sure that the matter will not be closed, seal or no seal. If you need to compare notes, then pair up with others who may be practicing Cauldron work as they will understand where you are coming from.

For an example of a softer working please refer back to the description I wrote earlier regarding the work with my Grandfather and note particularly the role of synchronicity as this is the language of Energy. When you have had a few synchronicities you will begin to see the power they contain and you will also see the expression of Energy and how it works through the Non-Material Self in order to bring new, positive energies into manifestation. Not all workings, however, are soft and the full potential of Cauldron Work needs to be examined. Let us take a more extreme situation and work it through to its potential, in order to demonstrate the power of the system. If I use the situation of any form of abuse it can mean many things to many people; in all cases, it will have deep impact on self perception as violation of this type will be all pervasive.

In a case such as this, the profile should be carefully built in the Cauldron. Yes, it will bring back unwanted memories, but these will be addressed in the process of transformation. Once the profile has been carefully built, cut everything into tiny pieces and light a fire in the Cauldron to burn the contents. Take your time and do this with passion as it will be more effective. The next step could be to urinate directly into the Cauldron, once it has cooled, on top of the burnt remains; early morning urine is best as it is at its strongest. Leave this to marinate for a while and then add some protective ingredients. Perhaps some nail polish remover to stop things sticking; some garlic to ward off the energy vampire; salt for cleansing and maybe a little bit of mandrake root to work the Magic. Maybe add a few healing herbs and a birch leaf to symbolize new beginnings. This sounds extreme, but the more extreme, the better it will serve you.

Let it marinate for a second time, but now seal the lid with Gaffer Tape; the last thing you want to do here is to accidentally spill the contents! Now find a suitable place to dispose of it. I would suggest a canal side sluice or something similar as these often drain into huge cesspits, which are not emptied very often. The toilet can be used, but this is rather too usual and it would probably feel better out of the home. The idea of leaving it somewhere very different and really foul has greater impact. When you let it go have a prepared rhyme to repeat as you do it, with the intention of just letting it go. This has nothing to do with retribution as long as the person knows nothing of it. They may feel the energy shift, but they will not know anything of where it has come from. Keep it this way or you will lose the Magic.

Take your Cauldron home and clean it with a strong solution of salt water to cleanse and prepare it for your next working. This is guaranteed to shift your thought Energy as it is a very powerful spell. If that person enters your mind again you will only have to think of where they have gone to produce in yourself a knowing smile. When you know the spell has worked seal it and move on.

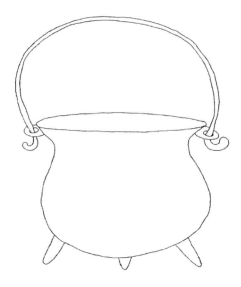

The Cauldron

We have now looked at soft workings and those which may be more extreme. It is for you to fill in the middle ground. Your recipes must be your own. Use whatever you have to hand and be imaginative; the two examples stated are only there as a guide, your ways may be entirely different, but the person you are seeking to help is you, so anything goes, it is entirely your choice. Healing is about making yourself feel as good as you possibly can and this feeling will display itself in your Energy field, making you more functional in the world of the manifest and facilitating a calmness of mind.

This state of being is necessary to attain before moving on towards working Magically in a meaningful way. To heal the Self is to get to know the Self by stripping off the layers of old paint. Once back to the bare wood, new finishes can be applied, but this time you will have the choice of the finish you want to use. What do you want from your life? Strip away the fears and insecurities and you will have more of a chance of finding out and when you do find out, it is only then that Magic will really begin to work.

Below are listed a few more techniques:

1.   **Poppets**. Everyone knows that poppets or witch dolls were used for sticking pins into to cause pain to another, but here we can put a new take on them. Make them from salt dough, clay or wax. The wax cases from little Dutch cheeses are really soft and malleable, they will all mould together into a lump. If someone is having a negative effect on you make an effigy of them as a kind of caricature. Spend time and effort to get it right. Give it some hair and pick out its features as the more detail you put in, the better it will work. It is very easy to get carried away with the detail as the more you work, the funnier it gets. Take a photo and keep it in your private collection and whenever they get to you look at the picture and see the humour in it. Do not show anyone else, it is your secret. Your overbearing boss will never look the same again! When you have finished, dispose of it carefully and respectfully. There will **not** be any need for pins.

2.   Amulets and Talismans. Amulets are protective and talismans are used to attract, but both can be made in the same way. Write the thing you want to protect yourself from on an amulet and write the thing you want to draw to yourself on a talisman, then reduce the word or sentence by writing each letter on top of the last. It will look a mess when you are finished, but if you are careful you can use the same lines for most of the overlaid letters. When finished look for a simple symbol within it and use that as your amulet or talisman. This can be on paper, wood, metal or anything else that is to hand

3.   Witch Bottles. Builders often find these buried in old houses. They are bottles filled with sharp things; such as pins, needles, rusty nails, broken glass and blackthorn spikes amongst other things, and topped up with urine. The idea is to hide one, perhaps under your threshold, to absorb any negative energy that may be coming towards you. They work well in themselves as when you feel negativity from someone you just redirect them into the bottle, then you, and only you, will have the satisfaction of knowing where they have gone. You can also create your own bottles or jars for specific situations. You can put anything into them that you see fit or they can be designed for a specific purpose. The only limit will be your imagination.

When you have a few successes under your belt you will find it easy to create your own recipes. Anything goes, there are no rules and you do not need exotic ingredients; a visit to the pound shop will yield all sorts of useful 'ingredients'. Bottles and jars, tin foil, lollipop sticks, wax crayons, thick paper (plain wallpaper lining is perfect), coloured thread, glue, paints and brushes or anything else that draws your eye. You will also find plenty of ideas in your kitchen cupboards.

All of your recipes need to be charged overnight in your Cauldron along with your intent, which should be written out carefully and left to infuse. Have fun with all of this and you will find it builds as you adjust your thought patterns. Nothing is too big to beat and the overall effect will be liberating. This work needs to be done prior to making connections with the Non-Material Self.

Moon Phase Correspondences for Cauldron Work

By timing Cauldron Work with the phases of the Moon a new dimension is added, use the following suggestions as a guide:

New Moon Magic. For setting out on new ventures or to initiate new patterns of thought.

Waxing Moon Magic. Use this phase to build on thoughts It is the time to develop initial ideas into workable structures. When you want to empower your workings, this is the time to do it.

Full Moon Magic. This is the most powerful aspect of the Moon. Use it to bring ideas to fruition. The Full Moon is the time of its greatest power and mystery, so meditate in its light somewhere out in nature to really connect with the timelessness of its Energy.

Waning Moon Magic. This is a time for banishing and ridding the Self of affliction. This is the essence of Cauldron

Work. Tackle negative thought patterns under the Waning Moon and allow them to wane with the Moon.

Dark Moon Magic. Traditionally the time of the greatest secrecy and sometimes used for dark deeds, but do not be tempted. Do the magic but make sure your intentions are pure.

Be aware of the phases of the Moon and work your rituals with its cycles. Moon Magic is a very deep practice, especially if you allow your inner being to connect with the energies of ebb and flow. Cauldron Work will be significantly empowered by this practice.

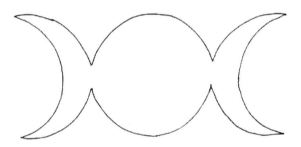

The Triple Moon

The Wheel and the Magic of the Sun

Sun Magic is the Magic of the masculine in the Anam Cara System. It is active and projective. It is about creating energetic patterns in order to influence future events. In the Tarot the Magic of the Sun is projective and represented by the card of The Magician.

Just as Cauldron Magic works with the phases of the Moon, the Magic of the Wheel works with the phases of the Sun. The phases of the Sun, however, work on a yearly cycle, in contrast to the monthly cycles of the Moon. It is, therefore, less instinctive and more structured, hence the distinction between male and female in the practice of Magic. Sun Magic needs to be highly considered and planned. It requires focus and objectivity.

In a group meditation I was part of, not long after the death of my son and a few weeks before Samhain, I was given the idea to make a wheel with eight spokes, to be decorated with the fruits of nature in order to represent the things I wanted to leave behind. It had been the worst year of my life by far, so I was willing to try. I gave it a great deal of thought and set about the task.

101

I cut a hub of ash and drilled eight holes around the edge. I consider ash to be my ancestral tree due to the connection with Ashby de la Zouche. Ashby probably means 'ash by', hence the association. I cut the spokes from oak to symbolize strength and whittled the ends to fit into the holes I had drilled. Next, I took some garden twine and wove a spider's web into the wheel.

A good friend and myself then walked the hedgerow along Napton locks and collected all manner of things to weave into it, fruits and berries, prickly things, leaves and foliage and a most peculiar red growth that neither of us had seen before. With a large bagful we set about the task of weaving and made the Wheel into a garland of the waning year. It sat at the front of my boat for a few days waiting to be burned on the Samhain fire to release its Energy.

It was to transpire, however, that I had got it wrong. One night I was woken up by thoughts in my head which I had no control over. It was highly distressing and so powerful I got up and spent the entire night attempting to get some handle on what was happening. At first my thoughts were entirely disordered and incoherent, so I tried to write them down in order to slow my thinking. As the night went on I underwent a whole wave of realization, particularly around the Wheel.

It was not possible to leave things behind and it was foolish even to try. What had happened had happened and no power in the Universe could change it. Why use the Wheel in this way when it couldn't possibly work, nothing could change; the Wheel had turned, events had happened and there was no going back. I experienced panic, my illusions were broken, nothing could be normal ever again. I was devastated and *alone. I didn't know what to do with myself. I paced up and down the boat and felt as though my whole world had caved in and the thoughts in my head erupted into a complete mess of anguish. Then came calm. I sat on the floor, tired and dazed and then came the thought to be positive, but what could be positive in all of this? I picked up the Tarot deck which had become my lifeline during this period and I cut the pack. The card was Cernunnos, the Lord of the Wild Hunt. I identified with it immediately through the wildness I had just experienced. I connected with him and sought meaning in my distress. The calmness moved into a new phase and my thoughts returned to the Wheel. I **knew** it could be used for the good. The past cannot be changed, but new potentials exist, if they can be found.*

I had tapped into something, a potential inspired by Cernunnos. I waited and kept my sense of calm until the realisation of meaning returned. Each spoke should represent a new potential, something to strive for, it was just about finding them. As the night went on each spoke did become a positive; a thing within itself. Death is not death, but a new beginning. My grief could not change, but life was with me and it was for me to find my way forward, not by denial, but by active means. What had happened was now a part of me and always would be and it needed to become a strength rather than a weakness.

Each of those spokes became a potential of strength and nothing was left behind. Grief and loss would be a part of me now, but must be used in a positive way. It was a beginning. New thoughts had grown from chaos, each one was written into my journal and over the course of the following year they were acted upon and each bore fruit. It was a long way up, but the spokes of my Wheel became the rungs of the ladder I needed to bring myself back from a very dark place.

Each year I now construct a Wheel and each of the spokes represents a new potential I seek to work towards. On each of the eight festivals of the Wheel of the Year I review where I am in order to keep my focus; it moves me on and gives me direction as any good Wheel should.

Within the Anam Cara System the Wheel is active and projective as a means towards creating new potentials and bringing them into realisation. Each Wheel should build on the last and should work within the energies of the Wheel of the Year, the energies of nature. It is about creating patterns and working with them towards movement within the energies of the cycles of the seasons.

The Sun

The Wheel of the Year

The Wheel of the Year is the cycle of the seasons as related to the natural rhythms of life. This was a way of being for our ancestors, but in modern times our lives tend to be structured around modern work patterns, which divorce us from an essential aspect of our Self. In the past the vast majority of people depended on agriculture, creating a deep and natural connection with the earth and what it meant to be human; but in the present, economic activity pays no heed to our physical well being.

Winter is the time when nature is at rest. This is also the time when we need to slow down and recharge, but work patterns dictate the levels of our activity. How many of us seek to hibernate at this time? We even have a name for this, *seasonally affected disorder* or S.A.D. (how descriptive is that term?) We are denied our need for rest and recuperation and that may lead to illness and depression. It is hardly surprising that early February is the time when absence from work reaches its peak. We **need** that time to rest and restore ourselves.

When Spring arrives nature begins its transit back to life as do we. Our Energy begins to be restored with the return of the light and we begin to use it; we clean our houses! Spring cleaning is a natural process, we come alive and we want to renew. We want to clear away the clutter of the past, in order to make a new start on which we can build. We are full of optimism and we seek to create new circumstances.

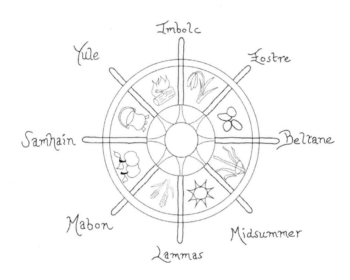

The Wheel of the Year

Courting is traditionally associated with Spring, it is the natural time for new love as it is the time of growth and conception This is the time when the birds and the bees are at their most active, the flowers return and the trees begin to blossom.

In Summer life is at its zenith. We want to enjoy the fruits of our labour as this is naturally the easiest time for us. It is the time when we can benefit from abundance. Life is never as easy for us as when the Sun is at its highest, and the fruits of the Earth feed us with vigour. Life is now a holiday, we have a respite from our labours as we only need to 'tick over' and enjoy the benefits. However, we are lucky if we have two weeks to benefit from this before we return to our stuffy workplaces. How good would it be to truly appreciate the benefits of this season?

Autumn is the reaping time, the labour of the Spring bears its full fruit and the harvest is brought in. The labour is hard, but the benefits are felt when the storehouses are full. This is the time to prepare for the hard times of Winter. We have food in abundance, but we need to make it last. We need to lay down stores to offset the hardships of Winter. It is an earnest time of work and preparation before the Sun disappears into Winter nights, but we naturally need to undergo this process. This is a time of satisfaction; we have catered for our needs. Now we have earned our rest.

What do we have by comparison? We have all year round work in the same jobs. We have all year round food in the same supermarkets. We have an all year round soulless existence in an economic system in which we have been trained only to want, and when one want has been achieved, we want nothing more than another want. Through tuning into the Wheel we can learn to be human again and we can achieve it through **simplicity,** but only if we **really** want to.

Correspondences of the Wheel of the Year

Samhain October 31st: The death of the Sun King. The power of the Sun wanes into the dark time. This is the night when the veil between the worlds is at its thinnest. It is a time to connect with ancestors and to welcome the souls preparing for rebirth. This is also the night of the Crone aspect of the triple Goddess. Use this night to burn the Wheel you have made, in order to send your intentions into the Otherworld, where it will find nurture. This is also the most powerful night for divination and realisation. Use the time to refine the plans laid out in the Wheel to prepare for the return of the Energy necessary to bring them to fruition.

Winter Solstice/Yule, Around December 21st: The rebirth of the Sun Child. This is the eve of the return of the Sun. The shortest day has passed and the light begins to return. The energies begin to stir, but now is the time for celebration. The dark time is at its end, but there is a way to go before the light returns. Tuck yourself up for the remainder of the Winter and enjoy the simple pleasures of warmth and rest. Anticipate the fertility of what is to come.

Imbolc February 2nd: Seek out snowdrops and wonder at how such delicate flowers can push their way through the frozen earth. The first signs of the Spring are beginning to stir. Now is the time to begin your awakening but not in too much of a rush, have a good stretch and some really wide yawns over the next few weeks. On February 2nd light candles in all of your rooms to symbolize the growth of the Sun Child. He is still as a young child and he consorts with his Goddess in her aspect of Maiden.

Spring Equinox/Eostre, Around March 21st: The Sun Child has grown with the nurture of the Maiden. The energy of the two reflects in the returning energy of the land. Seeds can begin to be sown in the newly warmed earth and the time comes to connect with the fertility of the promise of new life. Revisit your Wheel and plant the seeds you need to make it grow. You are bringing things into manifestation so feed and water your desires to allow them to germinate.

Beltane April 30th: The Sun King and the Maiden unite and bestow their blessings on the Earth. Life now begins to blossom and so should you. Be active at this time and absorb the energy of nature to empower your intentions. Be out in nature and feel the power of the earth. Be proactive in making things grow; the Wheel is your allotment and you will need to work hard in order to prepare it for the growth that is to come.

Midsummer Around June 21st: The Sun King is at the height of his power and the Goddess changes her aspect to that of Mother. The Earth is in full abundance and life is at its easiest. Greet the Sun King at dawn to express your gratitude. Your plans should now be well formed and beginning to manifest. The Energy of the Earth is with you to bring the fertility you need for your own growth, but it will only be there if you allow it to be. Open yourself fully at this time and let the Sun shine in.

Lughnasadh/Lammas August 2nd: The Sun King gives of himself in the form of the grain harvest. He is symbolically cut down and threshed before being stored for the Winter. He is John Barleycorn, the life of the land. This is the time of harvesting, celebrate and give thanks for the blessings you receive. The intentions of your Wheel now begin to ripen. They are nearing completion. Reflect on how successful you have been. Has the harvest been good or are there things you need to build on before the next planting? If the harvest has failed, review your practices but if the harvest is one of plenty, celebrate.

Autumn Equinox/Mabon Around September 21st: This is the last of the eight points of the Wheel of the Year and it represents the fruit harvest. It is the time when your own intentions reach fruition. Now is the decline of the Sun King, his power has been stored in the harvest and the Goddess begins her transition into her aspect of Crone. Now is the time to turn your thoughts to the work of the next cycle and to learn, just as a gardener does, about the pros and cons of the fertility of the soil. Begin the process of fertilisation now by working on your plans for your next Wheel. As the years go by you will learn from experience and eventually your garden will reach its greatest promise.

Creating a Wheel

My own Wheels take the form of small cartwheels without the rim and are made of wood. The type of wood used can be important. If you refer to the section about Ogham in these pages you will get an idea of the meanings of the trees. You need to work on eight intentions, so maybe match each intention to a wood that may correspond with it. For example, if you are seeking protection, rowan would be a good choice or for strength, oak would fit the bill. In this way, up to eight species of wood could form the spokes. Alternatively, the Ogham characters for each species could be burned into the spokes to include the Energy of each tree.

My partner prefers to make hers by tying four sticks together to make eight spokes, which is easier than drilling out a central hub. Both methods are equally effective to the operator. Different people have different ways and it is important to personalise everything you do that is Magical.

Find your own way of doing things as anything goes. It is the intention which is important. Perhaps use an apple as a hub and gardening canes for spokes. Cut a bamboo cane into short lengths and sharpen one end with a Stanley knife. Stick them into the apple and you will have hollow tubes to pack with the things you need to support your intentions (see the various tables of correspondences). You may even want to write each desire on a slip of paper to roll up and place in the appropriate tube. Just let your imagination run with itself and you will not go wrong.

The Wheel

Once you have your Wheel, bind it together with garden twine to form a web around it and then visit a hedgerow. Canal banks are ideal as hedgerows line the towpaths. Collect what you need in the form of leaves, berries or ivy to bind and weave, rowan berries to protect, elder for healing and anything else you feel that fits. Take them home and then weave your intentions, using the correspondences in the Ogham section to reinforce your ideals. Use colour, herbs, oils and perfumes,

Ogham fetishes, slips of paper or anything you feel appropriate. Finally, weave it with your nature collection and you will have a work of art. Finish this before Samhain and leave it to dry out.

On the evening of Samhain, light a fire somewhere outdoors and burn it. This will be hard to do after so much work, but it is your 'sacrifice'. As it burns visualize your intentions reaching into the Otherworld. The Otherworld is the natural home of the Non-Material Self and it is this aspect of Self you are seeking to nurture. **Know** that the intention is set and work throughout the year with meditation, visualization and dreaming to keep the intentions alive and to bring through realisations within your intuitive understanding. If this means changing things, go with it. The Wheel is not a tablet of stone and should never be treated as such. It may be that your original intentions transform, but this is the way it should be, the goal is movement and the finding of direction is **never** about limitation

Keep a record of everything you do. A sheet of wallpaper is good for this. Lining paper is a good natural cream colour and lends itself well. Draw out your wheel and mark it with the correspondences you have added, along with your intentions. At any time, but particularly on each point of the Wheel of the Year, take out your paper and work with it in accordance with the correspondences of the Wheel of the Year. On the festivals concentrate on where you are at and add to your large sheet any other writings you wish to include. This may be poetry, artwork, transcriptions of thoughts, additional correspondences, synchronicities or anything else you wish to include. You may want to add some Cauldron Work around it or include some further intentions. Keep records of dreams and visualizations you may have or any intuitions that come through. This is a living document and you need to keep it alive. Roll it all up together and tie it with string when not in use.

Alternatively you may prefer a diary or a Book of Shadows, but I will say I prefer the loose leaved idea as things tend to happen out of time when working Magically, making the linear approach rather confusing. At the end of the year it can all be made into a scrapbook by which time you will have it sorted in to some kind of order.

As you become more familiar with the Anam Cara System you may want to develop your work with the Cauldron and the Wheel with more complex correspondences. In the initial stages it is best to keep things simple and focused on intention, but as you learn more about different aspects such as herbs, trees, stones, perfumes, colours or anything beyond, it becomes natural to include these energies in your work. Do not move too far too swiftly as you need to understand what it is you are working with. You need to be connected with the energies before using them in your intentions.

It is often said that intention is all, and in the early stages it is enough. As your work progresses, so will your understanding of the energies of the natural world and it will be natural beyond this to include these energies in your work with the Wheel and the Cauldron. It makes perfect sense to empower your work with energies, but the empowerment is through you as a person. You are the catalyst through which energies transmit. Natural energy is, in a sense, passive, but in the working of Magic you become the projecting factor, it is your conscious intention which sends it forth.

Imagine you are building a force of energy. Collect as many aspects of that energy as you can and incorporate them into either the Cauldron or the Wheel. When it is ready, in the case of the Cauldron visualize it bubbling or spinning in the case of the Wheel. On its own it will remain, until you project it, as it is through your conscious and unconscious will that it will begin its journey towards manifestation. You are creating a thoughtform and sending it out to do its work.

A word of caution here, **be fully aware of what it is you are sending out.** You will be transmitting your conscious will, but you will also have unconscious motivations you may not be aware of. As you are a person of two halves; Material and Non-Material; it is the Non-Material side you need to seek a greater understanding of, hence the major focus upon it within these pages. Seek 'understanding' **before** you incorporate wider energies into your work, you need to know yourself and your underlying motivations in order to keep them pure.

Ultimately, if you do the work, you will learn the ability to create patterns in Energy designed to bring thought into manifestation through the medium of the empowered Self. However, where does the Energy go when it is transmitted? In simple terms, we can understand that it transmits from the conscious mind into the Material aspects of Natural Energy, the Cauldron and the Wheel, and then through to the Non-Material Self into the Energy field of the Unseen World. At this point a pattern will have been created to add to the whole and will return to the physical world in the form of manifestation. This may take many forms; synchronicity, healing, awareness, creativity, satisfaction and similar states. Keep it simple and it works, make it complex and you introduce variables, which may affect the outcome.

What about material desires and intentions? When reading books regarding Magical methods I often see suggestions to draw money and material possessions to the Self and also ways to influence others, in terms of love spells or healing. This type of Magic is not a part of the Anam Cara System. Anam Cara is based on simplicity, so material desires should be less important.

The lifestyle I live is simple and does not cost much to support. If I need money it is far easier for me to go out and work for it than it is to create thoughtforms and it is much more satisfying to know that what I have is what I have earned. For material goods, it is best just to expect what it is you need to find. Often they will turn up in charity shops or you will hear of someone wanting to find a good home for something they may have finished with.

In terms of influencing others in ways of love and healing or any other influence for that matter, there are serious ethical considerations to take into account. We all have the right to our own way of being, we have freedom of choice. We can choose our partners and we can choose our health patterns. It would not be wrong to say that poor health can be a chosen mode of being. Sometimes it is a comfort blanket in response to the pressures of life. Who are we to influence the choices of others? That being said if someone asks to be supported in matters such as healing, then that is okay *as long as they know, and agree to, exactly what it is you are planning to do.*

The Cauldron and The Wheel (Workshop)

The Cauldron, as a Magical image, is the womb of the Goddess. It is the symbolism of transformation and it can be used effectively to transform troublesome thoughts by Magical means. Use traditional Magical techniques, such as poppets, amulets, talismans, witches bottles, herbs, incenses, brews, and any other Magical technique you can think of, to create changes. This can be very absorbing and great fun. It harms none, so do as thou wilt!

The Wheel is a method of working through the cycles of the seasons using an eight spoked Wheel as a means towards making things happen in accordance with the energies of nature. The Wheel is the structure by which you plan, energise and actualise your deepest desires. This is also a great way to understand and connect with The Wheel of the Year.

This workshop is very much hands on and through it you will learn the use of a wide range of traditional techniques towards generating personal transformation.

Correspondences

The Language of Nature

In the practice of Magic certain conditions need to be met before effects can be produced; for example, in a witches spell various ingredients are used, much like a cookery recipe, in order to realise an outcome. If the ingredients are wrong, the dish will not come out as expected. In Magic, if the spell is performed using the wrong ingredients the outcome may be at odds with the intent. However, it is a little more complex than this, in that a cookery recipe is of the Material world, hence it is in the control of the uniformity of experience, whilst the Magical recipe is of the Non-Material world and is therefore subject to the 'shadow effect' of Otherworldly influence.

Traditionally, magicians and witches developed understandings of the energies of the unseen world through experience, and would use representations of these energies in their workings towards producing effects within their control. This involves more than a cookery recipe, as the ingredients are of mind as well as matter, as intention is the cornerstone of any successful Magical technique.

We have already considered the use of ingredients in the section on Cauldron Work, but now we need to develop on that concept to approach the more creative side of Magic. Cauldron Work is about self-healing and protection. It is about dealing with past or present situations, in order to still the mind in preparation for meditation. This is a very free-form, practice of Magic as it is instinctive. If it **feels** right, do it. There are no boundaries other than those of personal ethics. However, when we begin to approach 'creative' Magic we need to consider it as the practice of creating patterns of Energy towards a specific intention.

In the Anam Cara System this is the work of the Wheel. It is the creative side of the system and it involves tapping into the Energy flow, symbolised by the spiral on the top of the triangle at the centre of the Rosestrum. This process involves intuitive thought, centred on aims and directions, concerning future potentials. It is more structured than Cauldron Work and involves the use of correspondences developed on traditional understandings.

Correspondences are a major part of any Magical path as they form the building blocks of Magic as well as the means to interpret experience. They are **not** tablets of stone, but they are based on traditional understandings. They are easy to comprehend if they are seen as manifestations of Energy rather than material structures. For example, trees exist as solid structures in the Material world. In the Non-Material world they exist as shadows of images, but in the world of Energy they are composed of energetic patterns, which have been interpreted over years into the language of symbolism. By bringing these patterns through by meditation, dreams and divination the symbolism begins to speak to you and interestingly enough will manifest in your Material world to reinforce and empower meditative insights.

If you have ever consulted a dream dictionary you will have sought the insight of correspondences. I use this example loosely, however, as the correspondences of dream dictionaries lack the sophistication of Magical correspondence tables. Though based on similar principles, dream correspondences are decidedly more random. Dream dictionaries cannot be universal in their application as we all have individual experiences as human beings and hence our individual symbolic understandings will have differences. There cannot be a universal system of symbolic meanings; it must be individual, at least, in part.

This is why it is important to experience nature; for example, the energy of trees and how they affect us on a personal basis. We have the accepted correspondences as a starting point, but we need to experience them for ourselves, both in the Material world and in the Non-Material world through meditation and visualisation. We then need to adjust the tables to take into account our personal experiences.

In this way we can build our own index, corresponding with our inner understandings of the energies of the natural world and how they influence our Non-Material Self. This index will become a basis for interpretation of meditative insight, dreams and divinatory practices such as Ogham and Tarot. It will become instinctive over time. In turn this will provide us with deeper insights of the currents of Energy influencing us at particular points in our Self development. It is this Energy flow that works through the Non-Material Self to bring us the insight we need to move forward on our individual, Magical pathways.

The following correspondences have been developed using traditional understandings, coupled with personal interpretation, as well as categories specific to the Anam Cara System; such as the sections on Tarot correspondences and associations. Use the correspondences as they are on an initial basis if you are working with the Anam Cara System, but allow them to develop as your experience grows. You are aiming for a system which works for you and which accords with your experience.

The Planets

Seven Patterns of Energy

Seven is the number of Magic and transformation. There are 7 Days for each moon phase; 7 colours in the visible spectrum; 7 days in a week; 7 visible planets; 7 notes on the musical scale; 7 chakras, and the human body is said to renew its cell structure every 7 years. Seven, then, is a particularly special number. For this reason the correspondence table below has been formulated to emphasise the planetary qualities. Only the seven visible planets have been used to keep in tune with the Magic.

The planetary correspondences below have been reduced to a single word or phrase in order to reflect the essence only of the association. Look at the sequence of words for each planet and try to see the connections between each of the categories. It is only by connecting together the categories as a holistic concept that the actual pattern of planetary energy can begin to be understood. Your task is to add to the system and build upon it in order to develop it to include your own perceptions.

PLANET	SUN	MOON	MERCURY	VENUS	MARS	JUPITER	SATURN
QUALITY	Power	Reflection	Intelligence	Love	Strength	Vision	Restriction
COLOUR	Orange	Pale Blue	Yellow	Pink	Red	Purple	Black
METAL	Gold	Silver	Mercury	Copper	Iron	Tin	Lead
HERB	Marigold	Mistletoe	Star Anise	Rose	Nettle	Mandrake	Hemlock
TREE	Oak	Willow	Hazel	Apple	Holly	Ash	Yew
ANIMAL	Lion	Hare	Salmon	Hind	Wolf	Sow	Badger
BIRD	Eagle	Swan	Owl	Dove	Hawk	Wren	Raven
STONE	Sunstone	Moonstone	Amethyst	Rose Quartz	Ruby	Lapis Lazuli	Hematite
ELEMENT	Material Self	Non Material Self	Air	Water	Fire	Spirit	Earth
DAY	Sunday	Monday	Wednesday	Friday	Thursday	Tuesday	Saturday
SIGN	Leo	Cancer	Gemini	Taurus	Aries	Sagittarius	Capricorn
TAROT	Court Cards	The Fool	Swords	Cups	Wands	The Major Arcana	Pentacles
TOOL	Wheel	Cauldron	Athame	Chalice	Wand	Tarot	Pentacle

A note on correspondences. *In the tables within these pages you will notice seeming contradictions in allocations. This, however is not error as correspondences are not logical in their formulation. There is a certain logic about them but there is also a necessary degree of flexibility which needs to be recognised. Correspondences are used to structure the creation of energy patterns in your workings but they should never be seen as tablets of stone. The correspondence tables in these pages are designed as starting points only, your own experience will be of greater value as you develop your understanding.*

123

Ogham

The Magic of the Trees

When you begin to practice meditation, work outdoors among the trees of the material world. By connecting to different species you will become aware of the different energies of different trees. An oak tree will feel different to a willow. Oak will usually project male energy, whilst a willow will generally feel more female. Oak is sturdy and strong with the power of age. Its timber is strong and versatile, so it has a practical, down to earth type of energy. Willow, however, is of the Moon. It is nurturing, its long skirts whisper secrets into the breeze and it will only grow near water. Water equates with the emotions, hence the feminine associations.

All trees have their energies and it is by sitting with them that you will make these connections, even though the connections have already been made by others over many centuries. There has been a great deal written about tree lore, but one of the best introductions to trees is the Celtic Ogham, much of which can be found on internet sites. Don't take it on face value though as it is only opinion. Get out there yourself, engage with the trees and form your own opinions.

Ogham is a Celtic script based on trees. There are twenty species of tree or plant in the traditional Ogham and each has a corresponding 'letter'. Make it your mission to connect with all twenty and note the effects it has on the quality of your meditations. As you connect with each tree bring the energy of it into your meditations. If you are working outside with willow trees meditate and visualise also an inner grove of willow. In this way you will be connecting with the willow through the Material Self, as well as the Non-Material Self and will be making connections between the two. The triangle of the Rosestrum will be completed with the Energy of willow. Try to make it flow. Work in this way with the twenty species within the Ogham. Ogham can be used as a script and as a system of divination, but it is much more than that. It is important to connect with the energies of the trees by going out into nature to find them.

Begin by making a bag, it is always good to make things for purpose, and take it with you to different places where you will find trees open enough to give you a part of their Energy. You will find the trees easily enough if you go to the right places, but there will be special ones that really do 'speak' to you. Sit with them and open yourself to them and you will feel their Energies. The keywords overleaf make a good starting point, but it is your experience which is important. Your connection will become your understanding. Take parts of the tree, berries, leaves and twigs for your bag and keep it until you have made all of your connections. Also keep notes of your encounters. With each one you can build up your understanding by researching into traditional associations, folklore and mythology.

When you have the depth of experience you need to 'know' the trees, you can use the energies in your ritual practices; i.e. when working with the Cauldron and the Wheel. Introducing and blending the energies to your personal brews will add to the mix of what it is you set out to create. Ogham energies are powerful and can be used in the following forms:

Ogham Correspondences

Ogham Name	Tree	Keyword
Beith	Birch	New Beginnings
Luis	Rowan	Protection
Fearn	Alder	Insight
Saille	Willow	Intuition
Nuin	Ash	Transformation
Huathe	Hawthorn	Restraint
Duir	Oak	Strength
Tinne	Holly	Challenge
Coll	Hazel	Knowledge
Quert	Apple	Beauty
Muin	Vine	Prophecy
Gort	Ivy	Progress
Ngetal	Reed	Unity
Straif	Blackthorn	Fate
Ruis	Elder	Healing
Ailim	Fir	Far-sightedness
Ohn	Furze	Wisdom
Ur	Heather	Spirit
Eadha	Aspen	Endurance
Ioho	Yew	Immortality

Fetishes. This is the accepted word although I'm not sure if it is the best one to use, but it simply refers to the idea that every small part of a thing contains the essence of the whole. In this way acorns can be used to add strength, rowan berries can be added for protection and elder can be used for healing. The list goes on to include aspects of all of the Ogham. Create blends in this way for use in the Cauldron and the Wheel to generate Energy patterns you want to bring into your workings.

Fews. Fews are sets of Ogham characters and can be made from anything to hand. The simplest can be made of card and need only be the characters pencilled on. Wooden fews can be made with lollipop sticks or branches which have been whittled into shape. Characters can be drawn on with a biro or, better still, burned on with a pyrography tool. The best would be sticks of each of the woods to add the fetish element to each of the fews. One can be drawn when you are seeking a thought, or more complex layouts can be used for divination.

Essences. Take spring water with you on your visits to trees along with a few small bottles. Place a bottle of spring water in the tree you wish to connect with and sit and meditate with it for a while. What you bring through in your meditation will be contained in the water when you retrieve it. The memory of it will be yours, so it will be an essence of your communion with the tree. In this way different essences can be made from the same trees as your meditations will usually stimulate different feelings. Only keep the powerful ones and add to them 50% spirit, such as brandy to preserve it. To use them place three drops in a glass of water and drink them to bring those feelings back into your consciousness.

Charging. In a similar way to the making of essences, Ogham fews can be charged with the energies of nature. If you make a set, take them with you to special places and meditate with them to imbue them with the energies of place, trees, rituals and sacred spaces. Awareness of what you are feeling will become a part of the set and the energy will build. Your set will become highly charged and highly personal.

When I was working my way through the Ogham, visiting and connecting with the trees, I worked with a further five which are a later addition to the Ogham. I no longer use the additions, but still relate to one; Spindle. I had managed to make all of the other connections, but Spindle eluded me. I had never seen one, could not identify it even if I chanced across one, and I had no idea of where to look. I asked a friend at work who did a great deal of country walking if she knew of a Spindle, but her response was very much as my own. However, a few days later I picked up my post from my pigeon hole at work and there was an envelope marked 'Spindle' and inside was a sprig of leaves and berries.

I asked my friend about it and she said she had been at a friend's house at the weekend who just happened to be a tree surgeon. She asked him about Spindle and he said he only knew of a few in the area. While she was there a neighbour called with a sprig from a tree he hadn't recognised. It was identified as Spindle, at which point my friend's ears pricked up and she asked if she could have it. From there it found its way to me. This was a very remarkable synchronicity as, because I couldn't find Spindle, it seemed as though it had found me. I felt very satisfied about that; I must have made my mark in the tree world, so Spindle has a special place for me and always will have.

Herbs and their Correspondences

To further the principle of developing patterns in Energy towards effecting personal change, within the context of the Cauldron and the Wheel, herbs are very useful. However, the study of herbs is a field within itself, so a beginning only is offered here with a selection of twelve herbs to correspond with the Energy patterns of the Rosestrum. All of the herbs are indigenous and easy to collect.

The herbs can be divided initially into two groups, representing male and female energy respectively; and then into four groups of three, in order to divide them into their elemental qualities. Finally, each herb has been attributed an elemental quality in accordance with astrological correspondences. For this purpose, each of the four elemental groups, containing three herbs each, has been divided into three principles of **cardinal, fixed** and **mutable** qualities. **Cardinal** qualities are projective and outward looking, **fixed** qualities are static and unchanging, while **mutable** qualities engage in the process of flow. The table overleaf will enable an overview of this system.

Herbal Correspondences

Attribute	Herb	Sign
Cardinal Fire	Nettle	Aries
Fixed Fire	Betony	Leo
Mutable Fire	Garlic	Sagittarius
Cardinal Air	Agrimony	Libra
Fixed Air	Meadowsweet	Aquarius
Mutable Air	Mugwort	Gemini
Cardinal Water	Ivy	Cancer
Fixed Water	Burdock	Scorpio
Mutable Water	Ladies Mantle	Pisces
Cardinal Earth	Vervain	Capricorn
Fixed Earth	Plantain	Taurus
Mutable Earth	Mistletoe	Virgo

The work of the Cauldron and the Wheel centres on creating new patterns of Energy to correspond with the intention of the practitioner. This means the inclusion of appropriate additions. In the case of herbs, consult the table above to determine which would suit the intention best. In the case of the Wheel, each spoke may be empowered with the addition of one or more herbs. As an example; in the case of a spoke designed to bring about a practical transformation, it would make sense to choose a fiery herb with a cardinal quality. Consult the table above to see the herb associated with cardinal fire, which is nettle. Note also that nettle is associated with the qualities of Aries the Ram, which is a male, projective Energy. The colour association here would be red as an active Energy, so maybe also add a red crystal, such as jasper or ruby. If the intention represents a new beginning, then the number one can be added as a point of emphasis somewhere within the spoke. Ogham may then be brought in, perhaps to add strength to the intention, in which case Duir, Oak, could be added as a symbol inscribed on the spoke. The more that goes into the structure the greater the effect. When all of the spokes are woven together as a web include a sprig of oak near the spoke, maybe a feather to give it wings and a few mistletoe berries to symbolise the seeds of new beginnings. Do this for each spoke and the whole will border on a work of art, which is exactly what it is.

Let us take a second example to reinforce the idea. If the objective is to bring an emotional difficulty to a conclusion, a watery quality may need to be introduced. There will be a choice of three, cardinal, fixed or mutable. Cardinal qualities should be used to initiate, so this would not be appropriate as a conclusion rather than a new beginning is required. Fixed qualities are those where no change is actively sought; so we are left with mutable, which is centred on flow and finding its own level, this will be appropriate so look at the table to find Ladies Mantle as the herb. Now, when nettle was used in the first example we all knew what nettle was, but Ladies Mantle is not so well known, so we will need first to connect with the herb in order to make it meaningful to ourselves. Research into it, and find out as much about it as you can. Check out the Druid Plant Oracle by Phillip and Stephanie Carr-Gomm and consult books about herbalism for information, but overall try to understand why each of the herbs has been given that attribution. Go out and pick some of the herb or buy it as a dried herb from a supplier.

This being done, include the herb in your intention in its physical form; i.e. the Wheel and go on to add further ingredients. Mutable water is associated with the astrological sign of Pisces, so maybe add something fishy, such as a piece of wire bent into the shape of a fish. Add the colour blue as an indication of water and the number nine to symbolise culmination.   These physical additions will empower your intention.   When the Wheel is woven, add a sprig of Salle, Willow, to the web and etch its symbol onto the spoke.

When the Wheel is complete it will represent a great deal of work and preparation. On the night of Samhain it will form your sacrifice, and it will be a sacrifice when you cast your Wheel onto the fire where it will begin its work. Sacrifice is the practice of giving, as an act of faith, the greater the sacrifice the greater the return, so the more you put into your Wheel the greater will be the effect, but only if **you** make it so. You are not initiating a done deal with the Universe, if you want things to happen in your life you need to **make** them happen. The Wheel is only the beginning, you will need to make it turn, so at each festival on the Wheel of the Year revisit your plans and work out how far you have progressed and decide on the next stage of your journey towards completion.

Magical Uses of Herbs

Incense: Use a base of frankincense, myrrh or both and add tiny amounts of your chosen herbs to make incense. This may be used as a conclusion to Cauldron Work to send up an intention beyond your workings. Use about a teaspoon full of frankincense/myrrh, tiny amounts of herb or a combination of herbs and blend them together in a mortar and pestle. Use the correspondence tables to select appropriate herbs. Burn the blend on a charcoal block set in your Cauldron. Experiment with quantities as too much herb can cause bad smells.

Oils: Blend your chosen herbs into oils. Sweet almond oil is a good carrier. Mix herbs with oil, leave for a week or so and strain. Keep in small bottles and use to anoint candles or to add to brews. A little on the skin will keep your intention with you.

Sachets: Little, drawstring cloth bags can be made into a sachet by filling it with ingredients to suit a particular intention. Use herbs, crystals, Ogham symbols and general bits and bobs of your own choosing. Wear around the neck to keep them close to your heart while the magic does its work. Keep them under your pillow while you sleep.

Poppets: Poppets can be made in many ways. Salt dough is good because it is made of salt, which is used for cleansing; wheat flour for nurturing and water for life. The base is good enough in itself, but can be further charged by the addition of herbs and other ingredients to be baked into the recipe. Alternatively, use clay, wax or cloth. The choice is always yours.

Colour Correspondences

Red	Strength, power, lust, courage, passion
Orange	Career, justice, success, business affairs
Yellow	Learning, communication, intuition, thought
Green	Growth, fertility, abundance, health, plenty
Pink	Love, romance, nurture
Blue	Calm, wisdom, patience, stillness, creativity
Purple	Spirituality, third eye, inner knowing
White	Purity, spirituality
Black	Banishing, protecting, repelling, insight

Numerical Correspondences

1	New beginnings, starting out, planting seed
2	Choices, decisions, partnerships
3	Synthesis, the union of opposites
4	Stability, balance within the elements, structure
5	Balance of the four plus one, instability, change
6	Restoration of balance, harmony, renewed stability
7	Magic, transformation, movement
8	Double four, abundance, achievement
9	Three times three, completeness, rounding
10	Culmination, endings, the seed of new beginnings

The above correspondences give you structures to work with, if you choose to use them. Use them to create new energy patterns within the context of the work with the Cauldron and the Wheel. Add to them as your experience grows, but overall use your intuition. It is **your** magic and **you** want to make it work and **you** are the person best placed to make it happen, but only if **you** want to. Enjoy your witchery, but remember to keep it to yourself.

Workshop: The Magic of the Herbs

This is a day designed to allow you to work with a wide range of herbs to create incenses, powders, potions, ointments, oils and any other preparation you have a mind for. Herbs are extremely useful to the Anam Cara System for practices such as the Cauldron and the Wheel as well as preparing the conditions for successful ritual. This is a hands on day of practical alchemy with plenty of preparations to take away with you.

Section Four

The Magic of Beyond

Learning to Fly (thoughts in air)

Life has conspired to limit my spirit
And lock my free thinking away in a shell.
Choice now enabled has shifted restriction
But whither it leads time only will tell.

Movement is vital but thought needs to focus,
Clarity opens the way.
Look for the pointers, avoid the restrictions,
When working to learn how to fly.

Expect bumps and bruises from tricksters and muses
Beware synchronicity, watch for its traps
Follow your instincts but always ask questions
Never allow your free thinking to lapse

Be in control of your thoughts and your feelings
Know that restrictions can hamper the way
Awareness is based on your own understanding
You have your own life now so learn how to play.

BUT………it will only happen if you *really* want it to.

David Sutch 2008

The Magic of Beyond

We have so far looked at three types of Magic - the Magic of the Material Self; the Magic of the Non-Material Self and Natural Magic in the form of the Cauldron and the Wheel. There is a fourth Magical form which can be described as the Magic of Beyond. If we refer back to the Rosestrum we will find the first three types at the centre of the mandala. The Magic of the Material and Non-Material Self along with Natural Magic grow from the central triangle, so we can understand it as the Magic of the inside out. It is creative Magic that grows from Self and intention. We begin by working with the Material Self in order to loosen it from the bonds of social expectations and then we build up the Non-Material Self to strengthen its presence. With the two sides of Self united the potential of Natural Magic in the form of creating patterns in Energy can be achieved.

At this point it is worth a full recap of where we are at in order to fully understand the distinctions between the different types of Magic:

1.   The Magic of the Material Self: this is the Magic of simplicity and creativity. It works by changing consciousness and transforming the demands of cultural expectation to the satisfaction of Self expression.

2.   The Magic of the Non-Material Self: this is the aspect of Self neglected by materialistic culture. The awakening of this part of the Self, alongside the reconnection to it, is a Magic within itself as it works as a conduit between the Self and Natural Energy.

3.   Natural Magic: the spiral symbol on the upper point of the Rosestrum triangle is that of Natural Energy. With the work of the Cauldron and the Wheel there is interplay between the two aspects of Self and Natural Energy. The creation of the flow is the mechanism by which Natural Magic works.

4.   The Magic of Beyond: so far we have seen the Rosestrum has worked from the inside out, but when we get to this point, the Magic of Beyond, it works from the outside in. Look again at the Rosestrum around the outside edge and you will see the signs of the Zodiac. In turn each of the signs is set in its own elemental colour; brown for Earth signs, yellow for Air, red for Fire and blue for Water. On the black inner wheel are the symbols of the planets and their placements in the elements. Saturn and Pluto in Earth, Mercury and Uranus in Air, Mars and Jupiter in Fire and Venus with Neptune in Water. Again this is to do with correspondences, but we will look into this some more later.

It is enough at the moment to understand the Magic of Beyond as forces outside of the Self that influence potential behavioural patterns. For example, we all have a horoscope or natal chart which is representative of the planetary influences on us at the time of our birth. Detailed analysis of these charts is revealing as they often identify the roots of our responses in the social interactions of the material world and of our deeper motivations and desires. The Zodiac, it can be argued, imposes certain behaviour patterns upon us and is therefore an influence which does not come from within, hence it is a part of the Magic of Beyond.

We will also look at other influences from Beyond to include the Energies of Goddesses and Gods, meditational work in the form of a Journey through the Wildwood, The potential of Tarot as a tool of empowerment and the influence of the Zodiac itself, along with the mediating factors of the Planets.

The Magic of Gods and Goddesses

The Anam Cara System will work within the confines of any belief system, so the choice of any outside influence is entirely your own. This system is about Energy. It begins with the principle of a single Energy pervading everything in existence, both earthly and celestial. At the centre of the Rosestrum is the triangle with a spiral denoting Energy at the topmost point and it is this Energy we have been working with throughout the book. This Energy, however, has many different strands evident in all aspects of the material world. We can perceive that different trees have different energies and those energies are different from the energies of animals, plants, rocks, places, planets, constellations and also Gods and Goddesses. Ultimately all energies connect as a web of existence and it is that web we need to connect into, within ourselves, in order to weave the pattern that is the Whole Self.

Imagine that all of the Gods and Goddesses in existence are simply patterns of Energy personified by different people at different points in time and we will have a simple baseline from which to work. It is a useful exercise to make a study of different pantheons as it will become evident that many of the qualities of the Gods and Goddesses of different cultures overlap. This means that different cultures recognise specific patterns of Energy they seek to tap into with the intention of bringing those archetypal qualities into the Self. Personification of these qualities creates a focus for cultural consciousness in the form of worship. It is that worship which venerates a quality valued by the culture of which it is a part. In turn this allows individuals to call upon that quality to enhance their own existence.

This might seem a little sociological, and it is, but it is useful to us in the sense that we are working with energies. The Anam Cara System is about 21st Century Magic and the advantage to us is that we have so much information about so many Gods and Goddesses. The fact that all of them have been venerated at some point in time means they have been given Energy and that Energy remains within the web of existence. If we desire, we can tap into those energies. We can work with different Gods and Goddesses and we can invoke these energies into ourselves. Meditation can be significantly enhanced in this way as we can use it to connect with ancestral energies.

In my own practice I connect with a single god, Cernunnos, the Lord of the Wild Hunt, or should I say he connected with me at a time when my head was in complete chaos. Through that connection I received many insights and still do, so Cernunnos, to me, is my muse, I seek him when I need him, he stays within my consciousness and he reveals himself to me through synchronicity. I am always aware of him as the wild force in nature and I know of his unpredictability.

*My connection to him is natural; he is not a God I need to have faith in because I **know** he is there. It is not about belief for me, it is only about experience. As a person I do not seek to be wild or unpredictable, so his qualities are not what I invoke within myself, but I love it when my life follows his pattern. I want to wake up in the morning not knowing what the day is going to bring, I want my life to be unpredictable, I want to know I have a future which will unfold by itself and I do know Cernunnos will lead me there in his own wild way. He once presented me with a task to find 'the fixed point of stillness', and after much searching I think I have – 'All Hail Cernunnos!'*

I include that detail here because it is **real**. I have never found any solace in blind faith and never will, but at a very dark time this God aspect came to me unexpectedly in the form of experience as opposed to longing. He helped me through and for that I will always thank him. I have found my God and I very much hope you can find yours.

It is good to research the attributes of different Gods and Goddesses on the internet. You will find information on a whole range of sites and each one will be different in its emphasis. This is the way of it. The best you will find is detailed but not definitive. This is the way it should be. Use a range of sources to build your own description from it. This will be personal to you and will represent your understanding which, at the end of the day is all that matters. Below is one of my own as an example:

Reflections on Lugh *(written the day before a visit to the Rollrights when we watched an electrical storm in the distance which went on well into the night)*

It is good to get to know you Lugh Lamhfhada, God of the Sun. Son of Eithne, daughter of Balor the Fomorian demon king of underworld evil. A foretold prophecy of death by a grandson prompted Balor to cast you out. But Mananaan raised you to skill and ability and to manhood.

You sought the Tuatha De Danaan at Tara but needed to pass the gatekeeper. One person of each skill was allowed to enter but each of your skills was already present. Wright, smith, champion, harpist, hero, poet, historian, sorcerer, craftsman.....but who can do them all? Only you and so you gained entry. You followed Nuada to lead the Danaan against the evil of Balor. Balor had a magical eye that drew the life from all that looked into it. Trustee of the magical spear of Gorias known as the spear of victory as whoever wielded the spear in battle would be victorious but it was with sling and stone that you slew Balor. Triumph against the Formorians and the Fir Bolg followed. Eventually the Tuatha De Danaan were defeated by the Milesians and they withdrew into the Otherworld of Tir Na Nog where they became the people of the Sidhe.

You became associated with the grain harvest at Lughnasadh when you are honoured with corn, grain, sheaves of wheat, bread and other symbols of the harvest. You are the Shining One, handsome, full of energy and vitality and youthful. The late summer thunder is sometimes thought of as you and Balor sparring.You preside over communication, lightning, the harvest, protection, healing, the union of opposites, skill, success, victory, games, the market place, shoes, journeys, borders and boundaries, doorways, contracts and oaths.

The Magic of Tarot

It is because of Tarot this book has been written. After my first Tarot course the group wanted to continue together in order to explore the wider issues of Magic. It is from this point the present system has been created and it was also the birth of the Anam Cara School. Tarot will therefore always hold a very special place in the Anam Cara System as will the group who inspired it.

Tarot is most definitely a Magic of Beyond as the cards hold together so completely as a system. I have been reading Tarot professionally for some years now and it never ceases to amaze me how accurate they are. There is a reputation with Tarot I would like to address at this point which is the traditional view that Tarot is a system of fortune telling. The common view is of fortune tellers who see things in the cards and either say or just imply how fate will wield its inevitable fist - the future is revealed and destiny will take its course.

I consider this approach to be disempowering for the person being read for, as it is a case of the reader planting seeds in their clients' minds that are unlikely to have any foundation other than in the reader's imagination. Once a seed has been planted, there is an expectation on the part of the client that a certain thing is likely to happen, which may ultimately be disempowering as other courses of action may be neglected because of that expectation.

Properly learned the Tarot is a tool *par excellence* to work with and enhance the practice of Natural Magic. All of the cards have specific energy patterns which meld together in readings to generate a new energy as a collective in response to a question or a situation. The cards themselves, however, are simply pictures on cardboard, they cannot make things happen. It is the interplay between the images and the mind, which creates the Magic. A reading should never be by one person for another as this will simply impose that person's point of view. Readings should therefore be **with** a person and never **for** them. This is an important distinction as Tarot should be a positive means of Self empowerment for the person whose reading it is*, it should never be one person telling another what is about to happen.* All this will do is plant seeds of expectation, either for good or ill, but either way it will be disempowering for the person being read for.

How then does Tarot work? The answer is Energy, as with everything else within the Anam Cara System. When a question is asked and the cards shuffled they generate a spread of symbolism relevant to that particular moment in time. The spread relates to the thoughts present at that point in the questioners mind. If that person is not familiar with Tarot it is good to read with someone who does understand the cards. In this way various patterns can be pointed out, but it is how those images relate to the *questioners* mind that is of importance as it is the questioner who is seeking answers. The power of the cards is centred in how they stimulate responses from the deeper Self of the questioner as often we know what we need to do, but will not admit it to ourselves. The cards have a tendency to lay things bare!

The cards should also be seen as patterns of Energy. When laid out in a spread a competent reader should be able to bring out the main thrust of the Energy pattern within the cards. This requires a knowledge and understanding of the underlying energies in the individual cards and this brings us back to our old friends; Earth, Air, Fire and Water; the building blocks of everything in existence. However, the Tarot gives us another dimension beyond and it is this dimension that gives Tarot the edge over all other systems of divination. I refer here to the Major Arcana, which is also known as the Journey of the Fool.

The Tarot can be split into two sections, the Major Arcana and the Minor Arcana. The Minor Arcana is structured much like a standard set of playing cards with four suits and a set of court cards, while the Major Arcana is a series of 22 cards structured individually as archetypes, but together they can be understood as a story, symbolic of the journey through life in all of its dimensions, Material, Non-Material and Spiritual. It begins with The Fool, numbered O and ends with number XXI, The World. At the Anam Cara School, there is a series of three workshops designed to provide a full understanding of the cards over three days. The Journey of the Fool is the subject of a full day's tuition and will form the basic understanding of the requirements of a Magical path. This is the journey of the Self through life, so it is well worth the time it takes to present.

Easier to learn is the Minor Arcana and for ease of understanding this can also be split into two parts, the pip cards and the court cards. The pip cards are numbered 1-10 in four suits, cups, swords, wands and pentacles. The court cards are structured into the same four suits, but are labelled, Princess, Prince, Queen and King. All denominations refer to the Druid Craft Tarot which is the pack used in the Anam Cara School workshops. Each of the suits relates to one of the four elements; cups relate to water, swords to air, wands to fire and pentacles to earth. To learn Tarot effectively each suit needs to be understood in its elemental context within its numerological value. The numbers are important as each evokes a specific energy.

Through this method of learning, the values of the element and the number stimulate the intuitive meaning of the individual pip cards. This takes away the need to learn the meanings of individual cards which, if ever you have tried, is an impossible task and definitely not the way to learn Tarot. Learning the book meanings of 78 cards, even if you have a photographic memory, does not give you the skill to understand the underlying energies of the deck.

The court cards are different again. Many books refer to these cards as people, but with experience I find it more useful to understand them as families of energy. The Princesses are very much the energy of expectation, while the Princes are an immature, but dynamic energy. Queens and Kings are the mature energies of each of the elements. The polarities of male and female are also present here, but again as energies we all experience rather than as gender roles. Any female can experience the energies of Princes and Kings just as a male can assimilate that of Princesses and Queens.

To understand the court cards as families of energies is useful practice, but the main point here is that as fully rounded human beings we should be able to experience all of these energies within ourselves. Working with Tarot is an excellent way to develop our understanding of and the practical uses of each of these energies. To be balanced within the elements is one of the major goals of many Magical systems as it is from this balance that Magic manifests.

My goal in this section was to give food for thought regarding Tarot, but also to suggest a structure in which to learn the noble art. It is perfectly possible to learn Tarot from books, but do avoid trying to rote learn the meanings, Tarot is so much more than this. The Anam Cara Tarot workshops offer structured learning and practice within a welcoming environment. They also put you in touch with people who have learned in the same way and it is always good to compare notes!

Numerical Correspondences for Tarot

1.   The number One is a fixed point and provides a beginning. It is something given, a potential and a thing of purity. It is a seed unadulterated by anything other than itself. It is a starting point which needs to be nurtured before it can bear fruit. Alone, it will remain a potential that needs to be worked with, but where it goes will depend very much on how it is treated. Alone, it can only be pure and new as there is nothing to bring about any alternative within itself. It is like a brand new Tarot never taken out of the box.

2.   The number Two brings partnerships, choices, decisions, alternatives and different perspectives. It adds to the One in order to bring about movement. It is the beginning of process. Alternatives become possible. It can be a process of coming together as in the beginning of a new relationship, but relationships tend to follow a path that is not always

harmonious. Two can never be static, always needing to be worked with. The path will often be forked.

3.   The number Three is more than just choice, it is also the bringer of potential. Not the potential of the One, which has no movement within itself, but of the Two, which contains opposites. Imagine the Three as a triangle, the bottom two points are the opposites of the Two making the top point into the Three. The Three grows out of the Two as a synthesis of oppositions as from different perspectives new ideas can germinate. Not always though. Sometimes differences cannot be reconciled, but in this situation they must remain as Two.

4.   The number Four is the number of manifestation; the ideas of the Three become manifest in the Four. There is an extra dimension here as it includes the potential of actualisation. Four is the number of the elements, earth, air, fire and water, which can be understood as the fundamental building blocks of matter, so Four is the potential of stability and balance. Imagine Four as a solid oak table with heavy legs, solid and dependable.

5.   The number Five brings yet another dimension. If we keep the table analogy, it will become a table with five legs, a rather odd concept. The elements of the Four have an additional concept in the form of spirit. Imagine the Five as the pentagram. The new dimension affects the balance of the Four by adding a further point. Imagine also the pentagram as a person, with a head, two arms and two legs. A true pentagram will signify the perfectly balanced human being, but that is rarely attainable. Therefore Five is in the dimension of transformation. The balance of the Four has been upset by the addition of spirit, which is essentially an unknown quantity.

6. The number Six takes away the oddness of Five. Evenness returns and there is a sense of achievement in moving beyond the Five. The new dimension is the beginning of understanding beyond the inclusion of spirit. Stability returns, but it is rather tentative, there is still an unknown quantity, but growth has led towards a feeling of serenity

7. The number Seven is the number of Magic, the ability to bring about change. It denotes mastery of the elements and the ability to work between the worlds. It brings with it, however, the need to look within in order to understand the self for without this understanding the Magic will lack the power of insight. There is a challenge here opening the quest towards self realisation.

8. The number Eight is double four and so amplifies the stability of the Four. The flow of life is manifest in the Eight, but it is not as simple as the Four as the properties of the Seven are present in the Eight, so self awareness is a necessary quality towards its understanding. The eights themselves can be challenging on a deeply personal level.

9. The number Nine is the number of completion and completeness. Nine is a number wholly contained within itself as all multiples of Nine can be reduced back to Nine. This is true of no other number. We near the end of the sequence now, so the potential is actualisation. There is a real depth and power associated with the Nine.

10. The number Ten represents culmination and new beginnings. The One of beginnings is present in the Ten and it initiates the potential of a new cycle. This is the connection of the circular nature of life. As one door closes another opens. Life should never be static.

Astrological Correspondences for Tarot

The Fool is number Zero so is essentially separate from the order of the rest of the Major Arcana. The Fool is associated with Uranus, the planet connected with freedom, originality and independence. All associations are with the Druid Craft Tarot by Phillip and Stephanie Carr-Gomm

I   **The Magician**   Mercury.
The planet of intellect and logic. Male magic.

II   **The High Priestess**   The Moon.
Ultimately feminine with a dark side. Female magic.

III   **The Lady**   Venus.
The planet of love and beauty.

IV   **The Lord**   Mars,
Harsher, masculine qualities.

V   **The High Priest**   Taurus.
Fixed ideas of conformity.

VI   **The Lovers**   Gemini.
Two together generating choice.

VII   **The Chariot**   Cancer.
Emotion gushing forth.

VIII   **Strength**   Leo.
The strength of the Sun and the lion.

IX   **The Hermit**   Virgo.
The inner need for perfection.

X   **The Wheel**   Jupiter.
Expansion and optimism enhance the Wheel.

XI   **Justice**   Libra.
The scales of justice.

XII   **The Hanged Man**   Neptune.
The great nebulous mass. Who knows anything?

XIII   **Death**   Scorpio.
Ends and beginnings. Death and resurrection.

XIV   **The Fferyllt**   Sagittarius.
Limitless expansion.

XV   **Cernunnos**   Capricorn.
The security of firm foundations.

XVI   **The Tower**   Aries.
Raw, undefined energy.

XVII   **The Star**   Aquarius.
Of the people, humanitarian.

XVIII   **The Moon**   Pisces.
Ever changing.

XIX   **The Sun**   Sun.
The style of individuality.

XX   Rebirth   Pluto.
Transformation.

XXI   The World   Saturn.
The steady progress of limitation.

Tarot Workshops

This is a series of three, usually with two weeks between each one to allow you to process and practice what you have learned

Tarot One is the work with the Major Arcana as the Journey of the Fool

Tarot Two takes you through the Minor Arcana dealing with both the pip and the court cards

Tarot Three is your opportunity to put it all together and develop your reading skills

---

The Magic of the Wildwood

We now get to the true heart of the development of Magical Consciousness. Meditation is the development of the inner eye. It is the ability to walk in the world within. It is the means by which we meet our inner guides and where we begin to understand the Self. It is the beginning of a journey, a path through the Wildwood. Here we will encounter fantastical beings in a place without boundaries. We can walk in the mountains, swim deeply and without restriction in the lakes, we can delve into the darkness of caves and become beings of fire. We are in a place where the laws of nature do not apply. We can commune with the Fae, speak with animals, meet with the Ancestors and with ourselves as we were in lives that have gone before. Time has no meaning. Here we can be truly free. There is no social convention to restrict and there is no judgement.

This is the Otherworld, a place more real than this one. In the beginning it is a foreign land and a strange place, but it is a place of learning and as we delve more deeply into it we begin to come alive with potential. We bring things back and see reflections of the Otherworld in this one, but it is in the special places, the woods and the quiet groves, the lakes and the sea, the caves and the mountains, the animals and plants, as well as the Sacred places of ancient times. There are gateways we can pass through and shadows of the twilight bring us near.

You will be welcome there if you are open to it, but you will need to build your visualisation first. Your rational mind needs structure where there is no structure, so build one. It may be that you visualise your entry point as a grove of trees, maybe an island in the centre of a lake or a cave entrance. Whatever and wherever it is, it is yours and it is how you will enter in future meditations. From there you can begin to wander and find the places and experiences you seek. The more you go back, the greater your visualisation will be and the more broad ranging it will become.

Tuning to the Energies

To begin your meditations you will need to energise yourself. Sit quietly with your eyes closed until you are ready to begin. With your feet on the ground begin to draw up the energy of the Earth. Visualise it as golden light and slowly feel it entering every part of your body right down to your fingertips. As it grows in your head visualise golden light shining from your eyes and mouth. It shines also from your nostrils and ears. It glows from the pores of your skin, it fills you, engulfs you and energises you.

Hold that visualisation and hold your hands out with the palms towards each other. Feel a ball of energy between your hands. It will shrink and grow, just let it happen. When it begins to pulsate squeeze it hard and as you do this feel the light in your body forced out of your eyes, your mouth and the pores of your skin. The energy fills every part of you, you are bursting with it, you are a being of light, shining with the energy of the earth. All of the negativity that may have been in you and in your aura is burned away and you feel cleansed and healed. Now is the point at which you should enter the Wildwood

Walking in the Otherworld

When you are fully energised it is time to enter the Unseen realm. At first you will need to consciously decide on the landscape you wish to enter. My personal preference is a grove of trees and it works really well. Entry to this grove is between two standing stones as a gateway to new experience. On entry do not have any expectations other than a basic landscape and you will find things that are unexpected. Is it day or night? If night, what is the phase of the moon? What season of the year is it? Can you see fire, water, rocks? Are there any animals or birds? What types of trees, flowers or herbs can you see? Pay attention to all of the detail and write it all up when you return. These details are important as you are not looking for fantasy, but trying to develop your inner eyes.

Imagination in this type of meditation **is** the inner eye. You will need to learn not to direct your thoughts, but to just let them flow. The things you see and experience are the keys you will use to interpret your visions and the way to do it initially is to look into the traditional meanings, using resources such as folklore, mythology, the Ogham, the meanings of the Elements, the Wheel of the Year and its associations, the Druid animal and plant oracles, Tarot, moon phases and any other correspondence systems of your own choosing. This works well in the initial stages, but experience as always will kick in and your understandings will become more personal to you.

In the initial stages it is enough to just potter about in your visions, rather than trying to do too much too soon as you only need to familiarise yourself while developing a new relationship with your non-conscious mind. Go into your meditations, get used to recording and interpreting your visions until you are familiar with the process. You will begin to build up understandings of the things you regularly experience. In time your non-conscious mind will respond and you will need to allow it to lead you into experiences your conscious mind does not expect. When this occurs you will find pathways to follow from your starting point. Go with them and see where they lead. Always be aware of what is around you as you walk as this is important in terms of the symbolism and the meanings of your interpretation.

If we consider at this point that we are beings of two minds, one conscious and the other non-conscious, it helps the rational, conscious mind to understand what is going on. The non-conscious mind is the level beyond consciousness, but it is no less a part of our Self. We encounter it in dreams and imagination, but beyond that it is evasive and seemingly impossible to understand. At times we may be able to interpret the meaning of a dream, but more often than not they are unintelligible; that is, if we can even remember them. How many times have you woken after a very realistic dream only to find that it is completely forgotten an hour later? We only get glimpses into our non-conscious, but it is the part of us that likes to play.

Goal is the wrong word to use here, but it needs to be used for the purpose of clarity. It is our goal in this system to attempt to synchronise the conscious and non-conscious minds into some kind of working relationship. We can feed the conscious mind with seeds from the non-conscious and we can stimulate the non-conscious by allowing it free rein using active imagination. This allows us to work towards a more holistic understanding of the Self. This leads to greater potential and allows us the means to access deeper connections with our own Being. It enriches by broadening out our understandings of what it means to be human.

Feeding the Conscious Mind

In order to stimulate the mind and generate meaningful connections with the non-conscious levels we need to move beyond our normal everyday awareness. Open to experience and look for synchronicities in everyday life. In fact the synchronicities will find you. As your meditations enter your conscious mind you will see the shadows of your non-conscious journeys. The beings and situations you meet begin to echo in the world of consciousness. In this way emphasis is given to particular facets of experience and the path you seek begins to open. Learn to follow these patterns, some are blind alleys, but others lead to new experiences, ideas and nuggets of wisdom that accumulate until you are ready to piece them together.

You can also feed your active imagination with material to lead you into thoughtful meanderings. The folk tradition is very powerful in the development of potential. Traditional folk tales and mythological stories have a very real way of stimulating both the conscious and the non-conscious mind. Read the Grimm's collection and you will find stories to stimulate the imagination. They are often very dark and compelling and lead the mind into questions about meaning. Later tales are often just moralistic and their value is of lesser quality, but the early tales are of life and mystery, dark forces, warnings, analogy, enlightenment, impossible situations, guides and animal helpers. In short they can be journeys into the non-conscious within themselves. Look for collections of localised folklore, superstitions and collections of traditional tales. Eastern European folktales are particularly dark and intriguing and so are good and stimulating. Collections of myths are available from most cultures and are always worth reading too. In the Celtic tradition is the Mabinogion, hard to follow in parts, but full of intrigue. There are also the Arthurian myths that make excellent material for meditation.

It is not just books, there is so much media about to get you going, but it is not just media. Spend as much time as you can out in nature. Walk often and find places that stimulate you. A grove of hawthorn trees around Beltane is so evocative of the Otherworld. Blackthorns in full fruit carry you off if you allow them to. Buy a good book about the Celtic Ogham to verse yourself in tree lore and visit them often. Find the trees that speak to you and they do, if you open yourself to that potential. All of the time you will be increasing your awareness of the inner realms and your non-conscious will reward you with insights that may pave your path. Let it all happen, don't build in expectations but allow it to unfold.

Analysis and Discussion

This appears to be daydreaming, but it is much more than that. It is the development of alternative states of consciousness. You will be connecting two aspects of your consciousness towards a greater understanding of both, but you will also be reconnecting with ways of thinking that were unquestioned in the past. Modern society has lost the Magic that existed in pre-scientific times. We have become overly rational and rather black and white in our thinking. We have largely closed ourselves off to the mysteries of life and death and all that lies between. People in the past were connected very much with nature and the cycles of the year. Life was much harsher, at times cruel, but filled with mysteries and the unexpected. We have settled now for a rather sterile existence that is significantly easier but far less stimulating..

We have lost much and modern dis-ease has taken its toll. Instead of the infectious diseases of the past we now have stress related disorders, depression, workaholism, money worries, shopping addictions and the like. Modern society is easy materially, but the Magic has gone. Through meditation and work with the non-conscious we can, however, find ourselves returning to what is important.

How much do you actually need in terms of material belongings? Do we need to put ourselves under pressure with work to support lifestyles that are excessive? Do we need the latest gadgets and wall to wall TV? What is the point in it all? Everything is provided for us, all we have to do is earn the money to pay for it. Basically, we sell our souls to the workplace to pay for things we don't need. Modern society creates an illusion of happiness in its portrayal of the happy consumer, but there is a great deal more to life than this. Meditation is free, it is there when we want it; it frees us from the shackles of modern life and provides an alternative that makes us happier in terms of well being. We can leave the material world behind to concentrate on more important things and then we can go back to it. By working in moderation we don't need to stress ourselves out. We can provide for our needs quite easily if we keep everything in moderation. In this way we also have more time for what is really important. Leading a simple, low impact lifestyle allows the time to work on Magical consciousness, which is enhanced by simplicity.

The Zodiac and the Influence of Astrology

My favourite story of the beginnings of the influence of the Zodiac opens with the idea of a Creator. Who or what that Creator is or was remains entirely arbitrary, but the story concerns a Creator who has ultimate power over all things. The Creator made the decision to create human beings in the image of the Creator. There were other powers in the universe at that time, however, who considered this to be folly. These powers in the guise of the planets, were already in existence and they were concerned about the idea of unlimited potential within human beings. They expressed their concerns to the Creator by arguing that humans with unlimited potential would have the power to unleash chaos into the universe.

The Creator relented and agreed to limit human behaviour by exposing people to the constraints of the horoscope. This means that when a person is born they are subject to conditions imposed by the Zodiac and the Planets as they appear in the heavens at the time of birth. This is known as the natal chart and is rather like a fingerprint, a thing unique to every person. It is an astrological chart, mapping the positions of the constellations and planets, at the moment of birth.

Over thousands of years the meanings attached to the celestial bodies have become 'known'. Each planet and constellation has its traditional meanings, as have the interactions of these bodies in the form of patterns of energy, evident within the natal chart. With modern computer technology it is easy to generate natal charts simply by entering the date, time and place of birth into a dedicated programme. The difficult part, however, is in the interpretation.

A computer can provide the detail of a natal chart, along with a list of data relating to the specific positions of signs and planets, but what a computer cannot do is analyse that chart or identify dominant influences relating to a specific person, so it remains only as a list of potential, speculation and contradiction. To have a chart analysed by a professional astrologer would be expensive and would correspond only to that moment as the natal chart speaks to us differently at different points in time. The aim here really is to work with our strengths and weaknesses towards a deeper understanding of Self in terms of inner knowledge and outward manifestation.

Astrology within The Anam Cara System

Astrology can be a lifelong study within itself. Thousands upon thousands of books have been written going into very deep levels of understanding. For example, whole books have been written just on the influence of single planets or even the power of asteroids over our lives. To study astrology in its detail would take many years of dedicated work, but within the Anam Cara System it is only a part of a greater whole. We only need to look at the elements and energy patterns affecting ourselves. We need to look at the chart as it affects us and to locate it in our wider understanding of Self as an energetic being. Our work is largely with the Elements and their balance and our Natal chart can inform us of the state of play within our personal practices. The Natal chart need only be used in a similar way to a road map. We consult it when we need to and we don't need to memorise the whole thing. As we get used to particular routes we will have less need to consult the map as we will know where we are going.

In order to read a map, we need to know the symbolism and the format, so background work needs to be done in order to learn the symbols for the signs and the planets along with the elements in which they are fixed. This is not actually difficult to do. There are many internet sites containing this information which can be accessed freely. Alternatively a book such as Stephen Arroyo's 'Chart Interpretation Handbook' contains all of the information we will need to understand the mechanics of the different energies of the celestial bodies and how they influence the balance within ourselves. It is suggested that a text such as this should be used as a reference, as a detailed guide to astrological interpretation is beyond the scope of this book.

It is possible here to create tables to outline the information necessary for success in the understanding of the astrological component within the Anam Cara System. Our concern is with energy and how it affects us and how the balance of it can be adjusted within the Self, so we need to deal exclusively with these energy patterns.

As with all of the tables in this book, the information has been reduced to its essential form in order to work from a basic, but informed, understanding. Once the basics have been understood, it is possible for the reader to develop more detailed understandings of their own influences. Opposite are four tables each making reference to four main elements within astrology:

1. **The Elements:** the basic elements of Earth, Air, Fire and Water with their astrological associations.

2. **The Signs:** the primary energy patterns influencing the Natal chart.

3. **The Planets:** specific energy patterns existing within the wider patterns of the signs.

4. **The Houses:** the basis of human experience.

The Elements

Element	Meaning	Tarot Suit
Earth	Practical matters, material concerns, security	Pentacles
Water	Emotional concerns, empathy, feelings	Cups
Fire	Self expression, enthusiasm, action	Wands
Air	Thought, ideas, intellect	Swords

The Elements have already been discussed and the astrological meanings are much the same as the basic understandings. The aim in Magic is to balance the elements within the Self. We all have strengths and weaknesses, some of us may be predominantly water and consequently overly emotional, while others may be inclined towards air with a tendency towards over-thinking or too much mental activity. The information contained within the natal chart will specify the balance of elements at the time of birth. This information is a good starting point towards any work needing to be done regarding the elemental balance within the Self.

The Signs

Sign	Keyword	Element	Polarity
Aries	I am	Cardinal Fire	Positive, Male
Taurus	I have	Fixed Earth	Negative, Female
Gemini	I think	Mutable Air	Positive, Male
Cancer	I feel	Cardinal Water	Negative, Female
Leo	I lead	Fixed Fire	Positive, Male
Virgo	I analyse	Mutable Earth	Negative, Female
Libra	I balance	Cardinal Air	Positive, Male
Scorpio	I control	Fixed Water	Negative, Female
Sagittarius	I experience	Mutable Fire	Positive, Male
Capricorn	I expect	Cardinal Earth	Negative, Female
Aquarius	I rebel	Fixed Air	Positive, Male
Pisces	I escape	Mutable Water	Negative, Female

Meanings of Cardinal, Fixed and Mutable Energies

1. **Cardinal:** Cardinal energy is active, initiating

2. **Fixed:** Fixed energy is of itself, stable

3. **Mutable:** Mutable energy is adaptable, shifting

The information contained in the above table is a quick reference to the understanding of the roots of energy contained within the signs. This gives us a wider understanding of the complexity of the elements. Let us take water as an example; there are three signs based in water; Cancer, Scorpio and Pisces.

Cancer represents the **cardinal** nature of water, making it an energy with the potential to initiate action. Water has an extremely powerful potential when applied with force and will engulf all other elements in its wake. If a dam should burst the effects would be devastating, but equally it can flow with serenity and calm when allowed to take its own course. It is consequently unpredictable with an outward beauty, but its force must never be underestimated. This reflects people with Cancer strong in their natal charts. There is unpredictability about them implying a potential of moodiness. They are as changeable as the Moon, but they can also be engulfing to the people they like to be around, indicating a protectiveness towards loved ones. The quiet and stillness of water can quickly become a raging torrent.

Scorpio represents the **fixed** nature of the water element. There is a saying, 'still waters run deep', this describes the fixed nature of water. Scorpio is unlike Cancer in that it is more deliberate and less spontaneous. The keyword for Scorpio is, 'I control'. Emotions will run deep, but motives will not be obvious. With Scorpio strong in the natal chart there is a potential to hold onto hurts. Willpower can be strong and contained until the time is right to let it go. There is, however, two sides to every coin for just as Scorpio may hold onto hurts they also remember kindness and goodwill. It is a sign of secrets and as a water sign it contains serenity and calm, as well as the potential for destruction.

Pisces is the third water sign and it represents the **mutable** aspect of water. This is the fluid nature of water. It flows into every nook and cranny without limit. For this reason Pisces is associated with compassion, an ever giving flow. Cancer reacts and may gush, Scorpio will fix its intention, but Pisces allows itself to meander with a gentle flow. That compassion extends into the furthermost reaches, and is outward rather than inward in its intention. This may not be good for those with a strong Pisces element in their charts as they do not protect themselves in the way as those of a Cancerian or Scorpion nature and can consequently dissolve themselves in their ideals, hence the keyword, 'I escape'.

Overall water signs are invariably feminine in their polarity and they correspond to the Tarot suit of cups. These are people of the Moon, who ebb and flow with the tides of its waxing and waning. Lay out the suit of cups in the order of 1-10 and study the symbolism of the cards. Within them you will perceive the flow of water as it relates to life; mysterious, unpredictable, emotional, dreaming, intuitive, coming from a deep place with equally deep feelings.

Look now at the **Rosestrum** and turn the Sun of the triangle towards the sign of Cancer on the outer rim. Cancer is the cardinal point of water associated with action, a quality of the Sun. With this in place, the spiral representing Energy will be pointing to Scorpio. Energy has a fixed potential corresponding to the fixed energy of Scorpio. The third point, the Moon, will correspond with Pisces, demonstrating the mutability of the Moon in accordance with Piscean 'flow'. This will work on the Rosestrum also with the three elements of Air, Fire and Earth respectively.

As an exercise in astrology, see if you can work out the cardinal, fixed and mutable natures of each of the remaining elements. Begin with the information in the chart and build out from there. Use the above analysis of the water signs as a model. In this way you will develop your own understandings of the concepts.

The Planets

Planet	Keyword	Element	Tarot
Sun	Self	Fire	The Sun
Moon	Reflection	Water	High Priestess
Mercury	Communication	Air	The Magician
Venus	Emotion	Water	The Lady
Mars	Action	Fire	The Tower
Jupiter	Expansion	Fire	The Wheel
Saturn	Restriction	Earth	The World
Uranus	Individualism	Air	The Fool
Neptune	Transcendence	Water	The Hanged Man
Pluto	Transformation	Earth	Rebirth

Remember the story about the beginnings of astrology in which the lesser Gods and Goddesses or Planets challenged the Creator about unlimited human potential? Now we need to understand how the planets and their positions in the Natal chart limit the Native (the astrological term for the subject of the natal chart). Each of the planets has an energetic presence in the natal chart and their position will influence the character of the sign in which they are placed.

Let us take the examples of Venus and Mars. Traditionally Venus has the qualities of Aphrodite, the Greek Goddess of Love, while Mars has the qualities of Aries, the God of War, so here we have two opposites to analyse in our charts. If Mars features in Scorpio, in a Native who is a strong Scorpion, then the byword will be to watch out as the war-like nature of Mars will be added to the fixed nature of Scorpio bringing on the potential of aggressive control. Remember the keyword 'I control'. But if Venus were present instead of Mars, that tendency would be softened into a more passive outlook. I will leave you to think about a situation in which both Mars and Venus were present together; would they cancel each other out? I don't think so!

All I want to put across here is that a planet in a sign will influence the energy of that sign and that more than one planet will need a greater complexity of explanation. There is no need to go into the detail of this here as any good general astrology book will clearly lay out each of the meanings; Mars in Scorpio, Moon in Cancer, Sun in Leo and every other combination you can think of. The skill, however, is in the blending and the overall understanding of the energy of a chart and this is the part that computers cannot do.

Learn the symbols and the general meanings of the planets and practice the art of synthesis with the signs of the natal chart. It is good fun when you get the hang of it and you will develop a more detailed understanding of the elements in the process. If you have an understanding of Tarot, incorporate the meanings of the cards in the table to add to your understanding.

The Houses

House	Sphere of Experience	Element	Tarot Suit
First	Self	Fire	Wands
Second	Values	Earth	Pentacles
Third	Communication	Air	Swords
Fourth	Home and Family	Water	Cups
Fifth	Children, Creativity	Fire	Wands
Sixth	Work	Earth	Pentacles
Seventh	Relationships	Air	Swords
Eighth	Sexuality, Emotional Security	Water	Cups
Ninth	Higher Learning	Fire	Wands
Tenth	Position in the World	Earth	Pentacles
Eleventh	Group Relationships	Air	Swords
Twelfth	Transformation	Water	Cups

The next dimension of astrology is the Houses. They appear on the natal chart like the segments of an orange. Each house is related to a sphere of life. For example, the fourth house is the house of home and family. Consider the scenario when the fourth house is ruled by the sign of Pisces in which Venus is present. How would that differ from the same house ruled by Cancer with the presence of Mars? Imagine the sphere of the eighth house ruled by Scorpio in the presence of Mars; that is, if you can see through the sparks!

Natal charting is not rocket science and, if it is approached methodically, it is an attainable art. On the surface it is off putting with all of the symbols and geometrical patterns of the chart, alongside the constant need for reference, but if it is broken down into its skeletal form, as has been attempted above, it has a certain common sense about it. Begin with simple keywords until you get the hang of what is required and build out from there. Once the basics have been mastered it can become a very absorbing practice.

When you get the hang of the basic energies introduce yourself to the aspects, the conjunctions, oppositions, trines and sextiles, then you will really begin to have fun! Maybe also look at the Natal chart for the moment you begin a new venture, or even choose the best time to begin that project. Elizabeth I consulted her astrologer, John Dee, for the most auspicious time for her coronation. Hers was a very long and successful reign, so perhaps astrology is an art worth practicing.

Natal Chart Interpretation Workshop

Prior to this workshop you will need to give me your birth details of date, time and place. If you do not know the exact time try to locate it as near as possible and be in touch with me as I can work on different times in consultation with you to try to find a pattern relating to you as a person. On the day you will be given a copy of your natal chart with associated details. We will then work our way through a logical process resulting in your own interpretation of your chart. You will also have the opportunity to work with others in order to discuss the detail. By the end of the day you will have worked through a format you can use as a basis for the interpretation of other charts you may want to generate as a part of your work; for example, charts pertaining to the initiation of new projects.

Please note: I am making no claim to teach natal astrology in a day. This can take years. It is possible though to develop a working system designed to strike chords within you in order to further any work you may be doing on yourself within the Anam Cara System.

Putting it all Together

To begin the work it is important to develop a working knowledge of the energy you will be working with. If energy is treated as a single entity it is much easier to understand in the earlier stages of your journey. Beyond this, when you achieve an energy flow between your Material Self, your Non-Material Self and the Natural World you will reach an understanding of Energy, which will allow you to grasp its more subtle aspects.

There is an energy connecting all things in the natural world and it can be measured and perceived. Animals have it, rocks have it as do plant life, trees, water, earth and all of the heavenly bodies. It is a connecting force that permeates the universe. Animals have a natural connection to it and this can be shown by the fact that animals pick up changes in the energy of the earth prior to earthquakes. It is known scientifically that animals depart from areas prior to the impact of a seismic shift. How do they know? They pick up the subtle vibrations in the energy of the earth and instinctively move to safer places. Human beings cannot predict earthquakes, even with sophisticated seismic equipment.

Human beings, it can be argued, have lost that connection with the energy of the earth. We have consciousness and choice. Animals are more naturally connected with instinct. I think here about the story of Adam and Eve in Paradise. Consider a state of nature in which humans had a part. Everything was provided in abundance and the experience of being human was just to co-exist with the natural world. The story goes on however, to tell how humans took the choice of freewill over organic oneness with nature. Not sin, but choice. Old stories regardless of their sources can often provide food for thought.

Take it one stage further and look at the experiences of our ancestors prior to the development of culture. For thousands of years they lived a hunter-gatherer lifestyle in harmony with nature. This was not a hand to mouth existence as they were extremely good at what they did. They worked with nature very successfully, but ultimately chose to develop agriculture, which became the beginning of the end for that lifestyle. There are still peoples on the Earth who live as hunter-gatherers, but it is a way of life severely under threat by the dominance of modern culture.

Culture had its beginnings in the city states of Greece and Rome and developed over 2000 years to spawn the vast cities we choose to live in now. That choice, it seems, is no longer a choice, for it is our legacy to live as we do. After growing up in cities, it is difficult to live in simpler ways. We have basically lost the skills to live sustainable lifestyles, but all is not lost. We are very soft compared to our ancestors, but we have reached a point in the development of culture where there is a potential to reconnect with the Energy of Nature.

The positive side of culture, for those seeking reconnection is the fact that we have become a very affluent society. Even the poorest of us in the Western world are richer than our ancestors ever were. Britain, for example, is one of the richest nations on earth. We do not need to spend our time on the necessities of life as our ancestors were fated to do. Food is grown for us. The point is we have more time now than we have ever had, so we can choose a lifestyle that is conducive to connection with the aspects of ourselves that have become lost over the years.

The energy is still there and we are still basically the same species as our distant ancestors, so reconnection is possible, but we need to challenge our cultural selves in a serious way. The society we live in lulls us into passively accepting the position it determines for us. We are given the illusion we are free, but it can be argued that we are more controlled now than we ever have been. We are born free, but have become chained by expectation and necessity. The requirements of culture determine our life path and we follow. However, society has now reached a point where the free spirited among us can create alternatives. We are at a little window in history where those free spirits can reconnect with what it actually is to be human. We need to be vigilant, however, because our economic position as a society is highly precarious. The next economic disaster we fumble into may be the one that spells the end of our privileged lifestyles.

"What did you do after the economic disaster Daddy?"

"I learned how to plough, my son."

We will return to nature at some point in time, it will be a necessary conclusion to the excess of the present unsustainable, social structure, but it makes good sense to pre-empt that cataclysm and use the window we have to re-evaluate our lifestyles and our connection to what it means to be human. Ultimately it will be for the greater social good as change such as this needs to occur from the bottom up, rather than from the top down. Political systems are now so rooted in economic development that they are all but meaningless to the real issues faced by modern societies. Individuals are far better placed to stimulate alternatives, but always they will be at odds with dominant culture simply because the dominant culture bases its power on absolute control. We need to be able to exist outside of that control and that requires creativity in terms of lifestyle choice. It is possible, make it so.

The Tale of Hans and the Magic of Beyond

I wrote this tale about 20 years ago when I was deeply into the works of the German writer Herman Hesse. I loved the simplicity of his work and the fairy tale character of his style so much so I needed to try it for myself. Please read the story carefully as it forms the basis of the final part of this work.

Long years ago in a small town called Innsbruck there lived a carpenter. In his work the carpenter took great pride. Everything he made retained all of the love and skill put into its making to give his pieces a quality and character of their own. Accordingly, his work was in great demand and he was well known throughout the small town. However, he was not a wealthy man, as you would think of one so well respected. Though he had no shortage of work he would only work at his own pace and he only made what he wanted to make. His needs were few and the price he placed on his work was just the amount he needed to continue his meagre existence, no more and no less. This, one would suspect, was one of the factors which contributed to his reputation.

Hans, for such was the carpenter's name, was not a popular man. He had few friends and he always worked alone. The only contact he had were those he had to make in the course of his work. He was a quiet man and most of the townsfolk considered him rather strange, so tended to avoid him, except when they needed his services.

To order from Hans was not an easy task. He would never commit himself to a price, or a finishing date. One had to trust to his temperament, for if his spirits were high he tended to work harder. The harder he worked the more he made and as it was his want to charge only what he needed his prices dropped accordingly. The trick, you see, was to catch him when he was in good spirits. However, as Hans was so secretive it was very difficult to discern his mood. This led to much frustration on the part of his customers. For the same job one man could be charged twice what his neighbour had paid. When this occurred, no one considered the quality of the work or the low price Hans charged generally for his services. Thus many of the aggrieved would confront Hans, but Hans would not change, he charged what he needed, no more and no less. If he needed less he would charge less, it was a simple as that.

One particular quirk that was well known about Hans was his habit of disappearing for weeks at a time. He never said where it was he went or when he was going, he would just go. Mostly it was late in the night when his lithe figure would be seen leaving the town gates. When he returned from these wanderings everyone knew it was a good time to place work with him as he tended to be in good spirits. All of the people who had been kept waiting would be satisfied by the low prices and new customers would be pleased with speedy delivery. And everyone was happy, except Hans. He wanted no more than his simple life offered him. He shunned opulence in favour of frugality, though he always knew this was his own choice and could be abandoned at any time, but at no time had Hans ever abandoned his frugality. He had no respect for the rich and greedy, but always he worked for them and he always allowed them to exploit him and didn't try to escape the spiral. He felt very strongly that his place was in the town with the people, he could not conceive of any other way of life. He had been born in the house where he lived and worked and his father had been the carpenter before him and had taught Hans his skills and his pride. Now Hans was alone and he never considered any other way of life.

Hans was not considered to be a religious man. He never entered the church and his contempt for the priests was well known. Yet to himself Hans felt a deep inner need. He did not doubt the existence of something greater and knew more than most about matters of spirit. The only difference between Hans and the pious was that Hans kept his thoughts to himself. He interpreted the world of nature in his own way and disliked being told what to believe by others.

In his 30th year Hans took to wandering. Late one night when his spirit was low, he left his small house and wandered into the forest. He did not know why, he simply followed his instincts. It was early in spring when everything was new and inspiring Each living thing was going about its business fulfilling the tasks nature had given them. Hans watched this and felt a great stirring in his soul. He could see that every creature knew exactly what it had been created for. Each could perform its function with an apparently effortless ease, but what of Hans? He realised he did not know his place in the scheme of things. He had defined his own role and set his own goals, but now he realised how false to reality his life truly was. Hans then decided to seek for the truth and to find his proper place.

Hans searched and searched as he wandered in the great forest. He looked into the caves and under the stones. He watched the night sky searching for clues. He climbed into the trees and he crawled on the ground. For many days he searched, but he did not find any answers. He did, however, find a sense of peace and belonging. Empowered by his experiences he returned to his place in life and his workshop.

At home he felt high in spirits, for though he had found no answers he knew they were there. It gave him a whole new purpose in life. His work-rate improved and everyone forgave him his eccentricities. After a few weeks however, Hans' spirit once more began to wane and late in the evening he wandered off on his solitary quest...

It will appear odd to read a tale such as this near the end of a book about Magic, as it seems more of a beginning, but I will argue, this is a beginning. We have covered the majority of the Anam Cara System now and hopefully it will have resonated with you, but there is much yet to be discussed and Hans provides the basis of that discussion.

Unpacking the Tale

On first reading the tale it will appear simple, but when analysed in accordance with the Anam Cara System it will take on new meaning. So far we have looked in detail at three types of magic;

- **The Magic of the Material Self** in the form of creativity and self reliance

- **The Magic of the Non-Material Self** and the importance of inner being

- **Natural Magic,** the Magic of the Energy of Nature as a practical method towards resolving personal issues and creating new potentials

These are the Magic's of the inside out, described within the triangle of Being at the centre of the Rosestrum. We have also covered the beginnings of an understanding of the **Magic of Beyond**; that is, Magic which works from the outside in. On the Rosestrum, this is represented by the outer rings and the influence of astrology and the planetary energies. It also includes Tarot, the energies of the Gods and Goddesses, inner journeying and deeper connection. However, we have yet to paint it all into a single picture. The Tale of Hans will help us do this.

In terms of the Anam Cara System, Hans appears to be fairly accomplished. He is creative and self-reliant.. He is aware of the energies of nature, in that he understands that everything has its place. He recognises that he is different in that he has no awareness of his natural role, but he knows this is an awareness he seeks. He actively seeks his place and an understanding of Self in his journeying and this is the art of connecting with the energies of nature. Hans is also a thinking man of great curiosity, so there is a potential within him to understand the Magic of the inside out, Astrology and the celestial energies, the energies of the Gods and Goddesses, Tarot and the deeper connections of meditation. Even with all of this potential Hans had not fully connected with himself.

There is a missing ingredient here, a single factor not present and without it Hans will remain a seeker. What is that factor?

I will admit The Tale of Hans was written as a metaphor about myself and is true to my feelings at the time it was written. I was working as a teacher in mainstream education, was a single parent with two sons to bring up, a house to pay for and the day to day requirements of life to manage. I was also working magically within different systems. This was my secret life. I did not reveal it as it gave me a sense of personal identity beyond my roles as teacher and parent. I lived the frugal life, I had learned to connect with my inner Self and I made every effort to connect with the energies of nature. I taught myself Tarot and Natal astrology and had a real awareness of everything Magical. I particularly loved systems and worked at them until I had them cracked, but I needed something more. I liked teaching and I loved my family. I had many good times and was happy with my life, but always there was something missing and no matter how hard I tried I could not find it, but, like Hans, I knew it was there.

My eldest son moved into his own life and my youngest stayed at his mother's house at weekends, so I bought a small narrowboat. On Friday evenings I would go to my boat and stay out in nature each weekend. This was my lifeline. I was exactly where I wanted to be at these times and it gave me the strength to see me through the week. I did this for years and it served me well. I had a Magical life alongside a conventional way of being, but as time went on the pull from the Magical side became stronger and stronger. My youngest son went off to university and I was alone, although I stayed in teaching for some years after because it was hard to let go.

I became less happy and sought alternatives and made a plan to buy a narrowboat big enough to live on and then to rent out my house to give me a small income that would have been just enough to get me by. I held on to that plan until a time when I had enough money to make it work, but when the time came I could not do it, there was too much risk involved. For all I could live frugally I could not take the chance of putting myself out on a limb like that. Just enough was not enough. I castigated myself for becoming soft. I had been too long in the material world and it had caught me in its fears. Just as Hans denied the material side of life, he clung onto it, which was exactly what I was doing. On reading the story again I realised what it was Hans was missing and saw that without it nothing would change.

I carried on working magically, but nothing was working any more. I would read Tarot and realise it was pointless as I already knew how my life would be. I was a creature whose life was structured by bells and timetables. I tried working with the energies of the Wheel of the Year, but I had no control over my own energies as my year was determined for me by the demands of my job. I became disillusioned and unhappy. To break this cycle I sold my house and bought another. I sold my boat and put my energies into my new house, which I enjoyed for a while, but once it was finished I realised I was just rattling around inside. Nothing worked, my life was out of balance and the future was clear. It could only be more of the same.

Then it happened. I already knew the ingredient Hans was missing, but I had not applied it to myself. Indeed, I would not even admit it to myself, but there it was in front of me. I don't know how I got there, perhaps it was just by circumstance, but I finally took the plunge and resigned my

185

job. I was 52 at the time, not ready to retire, but I knew in my heart there was something more and I would not find it in the life I was living. I left that life on a journey, initially to nothing.

I was exhilarated at first. In the weeks after the school term began in September I would ride my bike around town watching people going to work and really glorifying in the sense of release I was experiencing. Then I would go home and enjoy a good, long breakfast to make up for all the mornings I had to make do with a piece of toast while getting ready for the day. However, there is only a short shelf life for experiences like this. I needed something more. It was not long before I came to the feeling of being at sea in an open boat without oars. A great void stretched in all directions. My life had been structured for me for so many years, but now the structures had gone. When friends asked about how I was getting on I would always reply, "great, so many things to do, I don't know how I managed when I was working". The reality, however, was different, I felt like the Hanged Man of the Tarot, nothing to do, but hang there and wait.

I was totally into frugality. I had to be as I had no earnings, so I made it into an art. I started writing a book about it and used it as a subject for public speaking. It was going well, people were interested and the ideas were relevant, but I could not make it into a complete system as it was about living in, but outside of, the present economic system and I was a person with a house all bought and paid for, which made me feel like a fraud. I got to thinking and Tarot came back into play as now I was really open to potential. I worked out, with the help of Tarot and meditation, a life that would work. The plan was to sell up, buy a narrowboat big enough to live on and tour the country to connect with people of like mind through my public speaking. By getting to know alternatives practiced by others I could share experiences and ideas, so I put my house on the market and tried a little internet dating to find a partner for on the way.

I found my partner fairly quickly but two weeks later came devastation, with news that my youngest son had died. My new girlfriend insisted I should go to stay with her, which was the best thing I could have done in the circumstances. I was away from the grief and with people who did not know of the tragedy. It was a surreal time in which reality took a different slant. I was looked after at a time when I needed it most and I will always be thankful for that. That relationship remained while my house sold and my boat was purchased, but as soon as I moved onto the boat the relationship ended by mutual agreement.

It was a dreadful time, but I feel this is where the Magic began, whatever Magic is. It seemed to happen out of time: The decision to sell my house, the plan for the new life, the new partner and then death. All had been put into place, the house sold quickly, the boat was found by a good friend, who just happened to have the same name as the boat and I have yet to see another boat with that name; I was looked after by my girlfriend and everything went through without complication and with virtually no effort from me. I moved onto the boat completely alone and it was there, out in nature, I went through my grief. I felt looked after, as though everything had been put in place by something beyond me, and during that period I continued to feel nurtured and never alone. I coped by walking many miles every day and through meditation. I all but lost myself in my inner journeys as they were so much kinder than reality. This took place over a six month period, in which so many synchronicities occurred as to make me feel I had really connected into something. It was a powerful **and** a terrible time. It was here I made my connection with Cernunnos and the Wheel.

Now, four years on, I can look back on those times with wonder, about how it all happened; it was not from me, life just seemed to take over and carry me through some really dramatic events. This is why I call it the Magic of Beyond. It did not come from me, I never planned it. I just had a few loose ideas in mind with a track record of not making things happen. These were huge, life changing events that occurred in spite of me. If I were to write the story of everything that happened, no one would believe me, but I know the truth of it and that is my reality.

With hindsight, I try to make sense of it and the only way I can, is to see my life before as a picture made up as a jigsaw. It was as though that jigsaw was completely scrambled into pieces and then put back together as a different picture, but using the same pieces. I am the same person I was with the same characteristics, skills and knowledge, but I am different, I have an inner confidence I never had before, because I **know** I am looked after. I have been through the worst thing that could possibly happen and I have survived. The pain does not get easier, but it has become less hard. My life is opening out, I have ways to move forward, but now I just seek to stay on my path and allow the future to be something I can grow into rather than control. It is exciting and it makes me feel alive.

I always struggled before with the notion of being on a path due to the implications of fate and destiny. The idea of a path seems to indicate a definite direction or a predetermined way. I could not accept even a hint of predestination regarding my own life, but now I see it in a different way. To watch a buzzard in flight, it appears to make no effort, but simply glides on the thermals, shifting with them. It cannot have any idea where it is going as it just flows. It flows without making any effort to determine its path and it lives according to what it is, a buzzard. In the tale Hans made the observation that everything in nature has its purpose, but that he, Hans, did not know his purpose. As humans, it can be argued we are species beings. We are a part of the society we grow up in. We are educated. Expectations are placed upon us and we develop expectations of our own according to the talents we have, but always in the context of the society in which we live. There is no 'one' human nature. Some people are passive, while others are turbulent; some act while others think and some are competitive, while others are not. Human society is full of contradictions and the range of human behaviour is so vast that no 'one' human nature is actually discernable.

We are all different and consequently there is no way to actually **know** human nature. We can however make some in-roads into knowing ourselves, particularly later in life. For me, it took the form of dissatisfaction with my life as it was. For Hans it was similar, but he **knew** there was something beyond worth striving towards. But for Hans, something was missing as I have mentioned before and his missing quality, as I see it, was courage. He did not have the courage to move out of the life he was in, as he would have no understanding of his life without its foundation of home and workshop, as this was all he had known. There would be a pointlessness about leaving it behind without reason, but by not leaving it behind he would be unable to explore his potential. To reach his potential he would need to cut himself adrift, basically severing himself from himself, to leave behind the part of him that had grown into the person he was. In the tale he was as two people, a deeper Self that was growing within him and an outer Self which was the sum of his life's experience. One needed to give for the other to grow.

What if Hans had moved away from his security, what would he do? Where would he go? What if he went through the process only to find nothing? Maybe he was better off as he was? At least he would have a foundation from which to search, but always he would know his life. There is an old saying, 'better the devil you know', however the spiritual quest is deeper than that and to find himself Hans would need to be radical. Leaving behind the shell of the person he was taught to be would allow the emergence of the Self he was seeking to know. It would be a painful process, but it would allow his deeper Self to make itself known. The split would heal, but there could be no way of knowing the potential of the outcome. It would take real courage for him to make that step but it would also be the only way he could find his answer.

The Tale of Hans has its background in the simplicity of rural life prior to the emergence of modern economic systems. For this reason Hans' decision was a much harder one than if he had been working as a teacher in 21st Century England. His life was simple and he played a part in the welfare of the wider community, so responsibility would have been a necessary consideration in any decision he made. He would have felt the responsibility of his place within his community. He would also necessarily need to cut himself off from his community in order to reach his goal, but would have needed to have been a part of something else in order to function as anything other than a recluse or hermit. Maybe he could find himself in this way, but to what purpose?

In 21st Century England these decisions are entirely different. My own decision to leave teaching was purely economic in its foundation. My fear was not having enough money to live the life I sought, totally different from the decision of Hans. 21st Century life affords us a standard of living never experienced by any group ever in the history of the world. We are affluent beyond affluent, even if we are poor in relation to other groups within our society. This affluence, it needs to be recognized, is based on the exploitation of people in 'developing' countries and the overuse of natural resources, but it is still affluence. How we respond to that is down to individual choice, but the bottom line is that no one in our society will ever starve, we are no longer ravaged by contagious disease and our wars are now fought by technology on the soil of others. Our health and welfare is looked after by the state and life in Western countries is materially secure.

If you have read this far into the book it is probably due to your own feelings and the need for something beyond. We live an affluent life, but it is not without its problems, as in the materialistic West, lifestyles are wholly materialistic with an almost complete absence of any alternative. For many that lifestyle works, which is fine for them, but for many there is a need for something more meaningful, particularly later in life. Challenging situations arise, maybe through the death of a loved one, divorce, absence of work satisfaction, feelings of meaninglessness or any other life affirming event. We are not equipped to deal with these situations with anything other than material responses, which simply don't work. Alcohol, drugs, retail therapy, television, internet vices and other addictions, may fill an immediate hole, but ultimately, they will have no lasting value. We have lost the sense of awe and natural spirituality our ancestors would have felt to have them replaced with meaningless, consumerist values.

However, at the end of the day you cannot buy your way out of tragedy or turmoil, as for this there needs to be at least some recognition of another dimension to the Self and the only person who will ever be able to find that dimension is **YOU**.

You *can* do it. It *can* be done. It is not earth shattering, it does not require deep, spiritual insight or the understanding of paradox. It is about the understanding of Self, a heeding of the inner voices and the courage to detach from patterns of learned behaviour that no longer serve any real function. Find your path and follow it without expectation. Allow life to unfold in its own way, but pave the road with your own intentions. Create your way and do not expect anyone or anything to do it for you. You are the architect of your own existence. Work on the blueprint, but detach yourself from it to give life the space to unfold. Magic needs room to work, so let go and allow it to happen.

The End of the Beginning

Samhain

The sun wanes in power
The veil between the worlds grows thin,
The hidden doorways are open to inspiration,
Travel deep and seek the subtle patterns
In the dolmens and the barrows.

The Hag holds power on this night of shadows,
Visions of death inspire our dreams and our visions,
The Gates of Annwn hang ajar
And the realm of the Sidhe opens with temptation.

The Elder is heavy
And the Yew delves deep into the mysteries of Ancestors,
Scry to seek the paths to the inner chambers,
Listen to the hoot of Owl and seek the Badger in his realm.

Obsidian night with full weight of Haematite,
The seed of the future is contained in the past,
The Death is the God but the play is with Apples,
The year is at end but the new will begin.

David Sutch 2003

Summary of the Anam Cara System of Natural Magic

1. The 21st Century Western human being is deeply connected to the material aspects of life to the virtual exclusion of the non-material Self, that is, the side of the Self which should be connected to the energies and cycles of the natural world. This is due to our scientific outlook and materialistic urban lifestyles.

2. The material Self needs to be played down by placing emphasis on reducing dependence on materialistic values and by becoming more creative in providing for personal needs rather than purchasing to satisfying wants. Recognise the difference between a need and a want and you will become more aware of this trait.

3. Go as far as you will in this practice but the goal is 50%. 50% simply means go halfway in the modification of the material Self to allow for a building of awareness of the non-material Self. The creation of a balance is what is required, half and half is a good balance. Too much on either one or the other will result in a lack of balance

4. To prepare the way for the development of awareness within the non-material Self it will be necessary to deal with difficult r words clear your mind for the positive and clear thinking you need for meditation by restructuring negative thought patterns through the medium of Cauldron work. Use also the yearly practice of the Wheel in order to reconnect with the energies of nature. This begins your reconnection to the non-material self.

5. Develop awareness of the four elements of earth, water, fire and air and work towards creating a balance within you, both materially and non-materially, within the practice of personal alchemy. The idea is to create an inner balance between the elements of grounding, emotions, actions and thought. Begin this process by acquiring a print out of your natal horoscope with interpretation information. The initial balance or what you brought into the world, should be present as a list of elements with their strength in your chart.

6. While you are reducing your material dependences and restructuring thought patterns, develop awareness of your non-material Self through meditative practice. The more your mind clears the more effective your meditation will be. As you meditate your non-material Self will begin to enter your awareness and will begin to interact with your material Self through synchronicity, intuition, dreams and realisation.

7. When you have cleared your mind enough to begin to meditate effectively, begin the practice of creating an inner world in order to structure your inner workings and to allow you to work with scenarios that will stimulate your non-material mind towards bringing deeper thoughts into conscious awareness. This practice will further connect you to natural energies. The non-material self is the conduit that allows natural energy to connect with the Self.

8. The object is to create a flow of energy through the non-material self into conscious awareness. This will allow the reconnection of Self to the natural energies of the Earth. This will also work with the polarities of male and female, the Sun and the Moon towards creating an harmonic balance within the Self. This is the completion of the triangle that is the Self within its connection with nature. When this state of being is

attained a natural initiation will occur, in other words you will have reached a point at which your life will be different and you will **feel** it.

9. At any point within the above, begin the development of an understanding of the language of nature. This can be achieved through work with correspondences such as Ogham, the language of trees, tarot, elements, herbs, animals, colours, numbers, moon phases, the Wheel of the Year, planets and the wider Zodiac itself. This should be based on a fluid understanding as what they mean to you might be personal and different from traditional meanings or the interpretations of others.

10. Within this understanding, along with the ability to research into further meanings, it will be possible to interpret inner journeys, dreams and intuitive realisations on the basis of traditional correspondences, balanced by personal interpretations, towards a deeper intuition of the inner workings of Self. It is through this symbolism that 'understanding' may be realised.

11. With balance achieved in the Self and the ability to draw natural energy into conscious realisation the Self becomes empowered, leading to the ability to **know** what the whole Self desires of its existence in human form. This allows the development of that knowledge into manifestation. You will **know** what it is you want to work for and you will be able to create patterns in energy in order to make things happen. Thoughts will have the ability to become things and things **will** happen. This is the essence of natural magic.

12. It does not end here as the Self will become an integral part of the natural world in its fully functioning human form. It will have the ability to work within the flow and will be able to connect with the current of a magical pathway. This is **not** a predetermined path but a flow of natural energy subject to the influence of the pattern of energy of which it is a part. The important thing is to remain within that flow in order to maintain equilibrium. The path is personal to Self and will accordingly be different for any who choose to take it.

13. The Self in its fully functioning human form is limited only by its own, self- limitations.

Recommended Reading

The Fear of Freedom
Erich Fromm
A psychological analysis of human freedom

To Have or to Be
Erich Fromm
Materialism contrasted with spirituality

Findhorn
Paul Hawken
An odd book about positive thinking and its benefits

Affluenza
Oliver James
An examination of a modern dis-ease

The Alchemist
Paulo Coello
How endings become beginnings

Voluntary Simplicity…
Duane Elgin
an American simplicity movement

Timeless Simplicity…
John Lane
good ideas, great quotes

Possum Living
Dolly Freed
How to live a respectable existence on very little

Sacred Celebrations
Glennie Kindred
Full of ideas about celebrating the cycle of the seasons

Ogham
Paul Rhys Mountford
An excellent Ogham sourcebook

The Druid Craft Tarot
.Philip and Stephanie Carr-Gomm
In my opinion the best Tarot on the market

Chart Interpretation Handbook
Stephen Arroyo.
Guidelines for understanding the essentials of the birthchart